WHAT CAN I DO TO MAKE MY MARRIAGE WORK?

12 Fundamental Criteria For An Unbreakable, Fulfilling and Satisfying Relationship

CHINDAH CHINDAH

Ten Things You Will Get from this Book

(in no particular order)

1. Fundamental proven theories to make marriages successful.

   In every aspect of life, basics are always important. In fact, I believe that the rudiments of marriage are more important than the improvements that most people are trying to add to their relationship. Without the fundamental theories of love, faithfulness, consideration, and godly consciousness, then taking expensive vacation together won't do much for your marriage. This book will build on these basic theories as the foundation of a healthy and lasting marriage.

2. Solid principles backed up by scholarly research and studies by marriage experts, psychologists, and organizations.

   Marriage has always been a complicated matter. With all the advancement of technologies and the dawn of new age philosophies, the secrets of having a successful marriage remains a mystery. There are myriads of principles that you can learn about marital union out there, but the best principles are those that results from years of studies and research. This book contains a lot of references from various scientific studies, surveys and academic researches about marriage carried out over the last decade.

3. Powerful ideas and concepts that will strengthen your relationship.

   Facts are important, but without weaving it to the fabric of ideas and concepts, then facts will just be dry as the Sahara desert. To further help you in the goal of strengthening your relationship, this book contains myriads of ideas and concepts relating to communication between spouses, valuing and exhibiting commitment, igniting the flames of intimacy and a lot more.

4. Practical tips and advice that you can implement right away.

   Books won't be so helpful if you won't apply the things that you learn from them. In fact, I believe that books are not only meant to be read, but to be applied to improve the lives of those who read them. In the same way, this book offers a lot of practical tips and advice relating to marriage that are downright useful and applicable any moment. You will come across a lot of these tips that will be proven handy to improve your marriage.

5. Reflection and discussion questions that will help you to assimilate the things that you have learned in each chapter.

Learning about principles, ideas and concepts won't be enough. You need to be intentional in reflecting on the things that you are learning. This book will help you to do that by giving you a lot of questions to challenge you to think deeper and reflect within yourself. Also, you can discuss and talk over the questions with your spouse to help you understand each other better and learn from each other.

6. Inspiring stories of couples who were able to overcome the complexities and challenges of marriage.

The secrets to a lasting marriage can be found, not only on the pages of a book, but also in real life stories of couples who were able to overcome and succeed in their challenges. There is no perfect individual and there is no perfect marriage. Every couple has their fair share of problems that threatened their relationship, but while some are choosing to give up and file for divorce, there are others who are rising up to the challenge and emerging victorious in the battle. This book is filled with stories of those couple. My extensive experience in marriage counseling has given me a unique platform where I can stand and see different kinds of marital relationships and I'll be glad to share with you that unique insight through this book.

7. Sound teachings about marital relationships that are easy to understand and apply.

While studying marriage can be too academic and may sound boring, this book will teach you in a way that is engaging and easily relatable. Though this book uses the results and conclusions of academic studies and research as a point of reference in certain points, the teachings about marriage has been simplified to make it understandable to any reader in order to elicit response and application from the readers.

8. Wise insights wrapped in analogies that you can relate to your marriage.

Good analogies make any complicated matter a lot simpler. In addition to the ideas, concepts and principles, analogies also help to provide a clearer picture for the reader. Besides, metaphorically speaking, marriage can indeed be compared to a lot of things – from the messy drawer of your spouse to the masterpiece in a museum. Analogies will help you to get the idea of the teachings without getting lost.

9. A step-by-step guide on how you can make the most of the book to further strengthen the foundation of your marriage.

To avoid confusion and to make sure that you get the most out of this book, I've included a detailed step-by-step approach that you can use while reading the book. This approach is geared to help you and your spouse understand the concepts better, find ways to help and assist each other, and focus on those particular issues in your relationship that need more time fixing. This will help you to have clarity in every step that you will take to strengthen and improve your marriage.

10. Challenges and dares you to aim to spice up your relationship with your spouse.

Sometimes, all you need is some dare or challenge that can help you to go back to where you were in the past. No matter how long you have been married, you can still benefit in trying something new in your relationship. This book will challenge you to try a couple of new things that you might not have tried before. I sincerely plead with you to accept the challenge and fully participate in all the exercises as required. This will undoubtedly transform your relationship and take it to a higher place of peace, harmony and fulfillment.

What Can I do To Make My Marriage Work?

Copyright © 2017 by Chindah Chindah

All rights reserved.

"What Can I do To Make My Marriage Work?

'' is a registered trademark of 4XL Professional Services Ltd
and Chindah Chindah

First paperback edition printed 2017 in the United Kingdom

A catalogue record for this book is available from the British Library

Printed Edition Hardcopy ISBN- 978-0-9957670-4-1
Printed Edition Paperback ISBN- 978-0-9957670-5-8

Published by 4XL Professional Services Ltd

1ST FLOOR 2 WOODBERRY GROVE

NORTH FINCHLEY

LONDON

ENGLAND, N12 0DR

For more information about special discounts for bulk purchases,

please email: publishing@4xlpublishing.com

Tel: 02071830366

Printed and bound in Great Britain

Legal & Disclaimer

The information contained in this book and its contents is not designed to replace or take the place of any form of medical or professional advice; and is not meant to replace the need for independent medical, financial, legal or other professional advice or services, as may be required. The content and information in this book have been provided for educational and entertainment purposes only.

Dedication

**I sincerely and wholeheartedly dedicate
this book to my friend, soulmate and beautiful
wife, Chimzi Chindah.**

CONTENTS

INTRODUCTION

"Your marriage reflects your inner self."

Chindah Chindah

Marriage is one of the most wonderful things that can happen to two persons. The idea of spending the rest of your life with someone that you deeply love and cherish is indeed a dream come true for most newlyweds. However, in recent years, the world has witnessed how the institution of marriage has been subjected to relentless attacks and is now slowly crumbling to its knees as more and more couples are going their separate ways. Marriages are being destroyed, families getting broken and hearts are being crushed under the pain and stress of divorce and separation.

In addition to this saddening phenomenon, once esteemed and protected marital principles that kept a lot of relationships strong and enduring are now being blurred by various popular beliefs and modern practices. These new ideas and concepts that supposedly aim to help develop a deeper bond between couples are resulting to a more shallow understanding of commitment to each other's spouse. Because of this, most marriages that we have in our present times are more vulnerable than ever.

Recent research and statistics reveal that there has been a decrease in the number of marriages and an increase in the number of divorce in countries in the European Union including Britain. Based on the most recent data available that were compiled by Eurostat, 986,000 divorces took place in 2011. The divorce rates are higher in several northern EU Member States such as Denmark, Lithuania and Latvia. This distressing statistics also corresponds to the increase in births outside marriage which means that couples are now avoiding marriage while at the same time choosing to cohabit.

A similar trend can be found in marriage and divorce rates in the United States. In the late 1980s, 50% of marriages in the U.S. ended in divorce and this rate has been rapidly rising ever since. However, based on a recent study conducted by the New York Times, the divorce rate is actually dropping and not rising. This could be encouraging for some people, yet this particular phenomenon can also be explained by the rise in the number of cohabiting couples. That is, the divorce rate is dropping because more couples are choosing not to marry. The rise in the number of cohabiting couples raises the question, *"Have we now found the perfect solution to avoid divorce?"*

Based on these research and studies, we can come up with a distressing conclusion. First, the institution of marriage is rapidly losing its relevance and importance in our society and second, to avoid the cost and inconvenience of divorce, a growing number of couples are opting to live together out of wedlock. Indeed, we are now in a time where marriage is just an option and cohabitation is the new norm.

But are we just supposed to accept these new standards of commitment and loving one another in the context of romantic relationships? Do we just need to accept the fact that the principles and ideas outlined to us by the Bible and even by those who came before us are now outdated, old-fashioned, and must be disregarded in our lives? Are we just to surrender to this new trend and admit that indeed, "marriage is dead?" Or we can still do something to fight for the true and lasting values and principles that make marriage last?

The Ideal Marriage

With all the depressing research studies and statistics that are being discovered about marriage and also with the ever-changing perspectives of individuals when it comes to their concept of moral correctness with regards to matrimony, the timeless and enduring truths about marriage is needed more than ever. And for us to understand the ideal picture of marriage, we need to go back to a couple of thousands of years ago where the first union of man and woman is recorded. According to the Bible,

"For this reason a man shall leave his father and mother, And be joined to his wife; and they shall become one flesh."

The original plan for marriage portrays the idea of a lifetime union. Thus, according to a separate verse in the Bible, *"What God has joined together, let no one separate."* A man and a woman who decided to bind each other in the sacrament of marriage are actually supposed to stay together until death separates them. Divorce was never an option in the original plan. However, the result of the fall has tremendously distorted the ideal concept of everything in our lives.

In not so distant past, about 50 years ago, marriages were also significantly different from what we now have. For instance, in the 1950s marriages were considered to be an integral component of starting out in life; normally after High School. The wedlock during that time was also not that complicated because spouses have generic and defined role in their marriage. The husband was the one who isl expected to work and provide for the financial needs of the family, while the wife was supposed to stay at home, take care of the chores and the children and support her husband on the side. The divorce rate during that time was at 23% and majority of the people didn't see divorce as normal, rather it was associated with failure.

In today's marriage, the role of husband and wife is not that simple. Depending on the needs of the family, both spouses might opt to work separately in order to provide the financial support needed. Most people now choose to marry at a later age, while a growing number of young men and women now decide not to get married at all, but instead to just cohabit. The complexity of our modern life greatly affected the values that we have when it comes to marriage. The same technology that enables people to get connected even when they are miles away, is the same advancement in our lives that have caused couples to stay apart. Now, the divorce rate is ranging from 40% to 50% with the society seeing divorce as a normal way of life and as essential to survival.

An insightful story captures this idea of comparing the marriages in the past to the marriages that we see in the society now. An old lady was chatting to her young granddaughter who was distraught after receiving the Divorce Letter earlier in the morning. The young lady said, *"How did you and Grandpa manage to stay together that long?"* To which her grandmother kindly responded, *"My child, your Grandpa and I were born in a time where if something is broken, we fix it. Not throw it away."*

Nowadays, to catch a glimpse of an ideal marriage is like seeing a rare diamond among a vast heap of stones. It's priceless; it's an amazing experience; It's beautiful. However, what most people do not understand is that the ideal marriage is not perfect- yes, you heard it right. The ideal marriage is not perfect because no marriage can ever be perfect. A marriage is a union of two imperfect individuals with their own flaws and shortcomings. And when you brought two flawed persons to be joined for life, then of course, you will come up also with a flawed marriage. But what makes this imperfect union ideal is the virtue of accepting each other wholly in spite of the shortcoming of each other. I know it's more complicated than that but that is the basic idea.

The ideal marriage is still messy, but the partners choose to see the beauty in their companion. Sometimes, the ideal marriage is outright ugly, but the couples inside the marriage focus on the things that they admire in each other. It is not to say that they ignore the glaring problem that is staring them right in the face. They acknowledge it and do their best to solve it, but they are not letting their love and commitment to each other be overshadowed by disappointments, pain, and problems. You see, the ideal marriage is not ideal because it has no flaws; the ideal marriage is ideal because there is love, the true kind of love. It is the kind of love that the Apostle Paul speaks about in 1 Corinthians 13, where the Bible says:

Love is patient, love is kind. It does not envy, it does not boast, it is not proud. It does not dishonor others, it is not

self-seeking, it is not easily angered, it keeps no record of
wrongs. Love does not delight in evil but rejoices with the
truth. It always protects, always trusts, always hopes,
always perseveres.

Bridging the Gap

Now, you might be thinking, *"You know what, everything that*
you are saying here is wonderful, but you don't know our
marriage. You don't know the things that happen to us that destroy
our love for each other. You don't know what my spouse said and
did to me. You don't understand the pain and the heartache that
we inflict on each other. Everything that you say here is great, but
you don't know a thing about our marriage. In fact, I believe that
no one can save our marriage."

If that is what you are thinking, then first, let me say sorry! I
understand that marriage can sometimes be painful and downright
agonizing. However, I also believe that there is still hope for a lot
of couples out there and divorce is not the sole solution in order to
escape the pain. In fact, it is my personal conviction that you can
help your marriage to be divorce-proof. But it will happen only if
you will choose to do it.

The goal of this book is to help you have some directions on
how to do it. This manuscript is filled with a lot of useful insights,
tips and practical techniques that you can implement right away to
improve your marriage in the first hour of reading it. Yes, if you
would be brave enough to try what I will teach you here, then I can
guarantee that you can improve some aspects of your marriage
right away. Think about this, what if you will spend five minutes at
this very moment to compliment your spouse, will it make a
difference? Or try to spend ten minutes right now and write a
simple and short note expressing your admiration and love for your
husband or wife, will it make a difference? Or just spend fifteen
minutes at this moment and get a piece of paper to list down all the
good qualities that you love about your spouse, will it make a
difference?

You see, everything hangs on the actions that you are willing to take. And yes, I understand that it might not be easy for you, especially if you have deep feelings of resentment that you have cultivated over the years. It might also be difficult if you have not felt that rushing love for years now or you didn't receive any admiration and appreciation from your spouse over the years. But just for the sake of argument, will doing good to your spouse today make a difference in your marriage – no matter how small it is?

The Twelve

From my experience with marriage and based on the things that I learned over the years. I realised that there are 12 basic components of a successful marriage. These are the principles and concepts that can help you to make your marriage work. I want to call this the *"12 Fundamental Criteria for an Unbreakable, Fulfilling, and Satisfying Relationship."* I know that's a mouthful, so let just call it the *"Twelve."* The *Twelve* are fundamental because every successful marriage that we know is built on these criteria. Also, if you are having trouble with your marriage, then you can spot it by evaluating your relationship based on the *Twelve*. And if you are aiming to improve your marriage and make it more satisfying and fulfilling for you and your partner, then you need to improve on the *Twelve*. The *Twelve* are the basics, the foundation, and the precise principles that you need to work on to have an ideal marriage. Let me introduce you to the *Twelve* right now. Each criterion will be discussed in greater depth later in this book,

1. *Commitment* – standing by your spouse no matter what problem comes. This is the essence of unconditional love that every married partner needs.
2. *Communication* – talking deeply and expressing your true self in a way that you are growing in knowledge with each other.
3. *Consideration* – giving allowance to each other's imperfection.
4. *Commendation* – the art of appreciating each other and providing mutual support to individual pursuits of spouses.
5. *Correction* – lovingly helping your spouse to make the necessary improvements in character and attitude. Also about

taking responsibility for the mistakes to avoid blaming each other.

6. *Connection* – investing time to connect with each other on a deeper level. It is also about seeing things on each other's perspective in order to minimize misunderstanding.

7. *Consummation* – expressing love using the medium of sexual intimacy.

8. *Conservation* – mostly about being wise in spending money. It is also about making financial decisions together.

9. *Confession* – things will go wrong in marriage. And having a strong foundation of confession and forgiveness will help to weather these storms.

10. *Continuation* – intentionally improving yourself in different aspects of your life. Partners should also become partners for personal growth and development.

11. *Completion* – marriage must be complete and should not end in divorce. Complete the vow that spouses made to each other namely, *'Til death do us part."*

12. *Consciousness* – having the awareness that couples need Divine help and supernatural support at all times. God must be in the center of the relationship in order to make it stronger.

I know, the *Twelve* is quite a long list, but believe me, mastering these fundamental criteria will greatly improve your relationship with each other. Just imagine being skilled in the criterion of *Communication.* Every day, you engage in a meaningful and deep conversation with your spouse. You genuinely desire to know more about her and in spite of the years that have gone by, you still have this insatiable hunger to learn more of her fears, aspirations, and dreams. What good will it do to your marriage? Or think about applying and mastering the criterion of *Conservation.* According to studies, one of the most common problems that cause heated arguments between married partners is the issue of money. But what if you can virtually eliminate this problem because you are in-sync when it comes to financial decisions?

Remember, the *Twelve* is fundamental. These criteria are the basic components for a healthy, functional, and lasting marriage. Get it right, and I can guarantee that you will have the tools that you need to weather any storm that might come in your marriage. Get it wrong or neglect it, and you will see your marriage slowly crumble before your very eyes.

How to Get the Most from this Book?

As I have mentioned before, this book is full of useful insights and practical tips that you can implement right away if you want to improve your marriage. However, for you and your spouse (*Yes, I recommend that both of you read it together*) to get the most of this book, then I have some suggestions:

1. Read the book from start to finish rapidly

If it is possible, set aside chunks of time in your schedule to read the book together. If it is also possible, try to finish the book in a week together with your spouse. The goal of reading the whole material as quickly as possible is for you to get a *feel* of the things that you will learn in this book. Also, by trying to go over the whole material, you can immediately identify the area of your marriage that needs more work from you and your partner. For instance, if upon reading the whole book, you realise that your main problem right now is in the fundamental criterion of *Commendation,* then you can plan to work on it right away. Again, the goal of reading the book rapidly is to get a feel and identify the area that must be addressed immediately.

2. Based on your initial reading, rank the Twelve on the basis of what needs immediate attention

After getting a *feel* of the things that you are about to learn, now I suggest that you list down the *Twelve* and arrange them in a way that reflects your priority. What I mean is you rank the *Twelve* based from worst to good, with the worst area being the top priority. So if you realise that you rarely talk to one another, then perhaps you need to fix that immediately. Put *Communication* as your Number 1 Priority. From there arrange the other criteria from top to bottom on the basis of their descending priority in your marriage. You can also arrange the *Twelve* based on the most logical approach that you can think of. If you are a Christian, then you might want to start with the fundamental criterion of *Consciousness,* especially if you realise that God is not at the centre of your relationship.

3. Set aside a whole week to work on each criterion

Indeed, working on the *Twelve* might be a daunting task. You can't effectively solve your problem by focusing on so many things at the same time and any effort to spread yourself thin over multiple issues could be counterproductive. We cannot take that huge risk when it comes to your marriage, so I just suggest that you work on each fundamental criterion per week. For instance, if after reading the whole material for the first time, you were able to ascertain that you truly need divine help, then just focus on that criterion for a whole week. Read through the chapter that discusses that criterion and do the suggested tasks found in the workbook. Do this for one week and then move to the next criterion the following week until you complete all the *Twelve* criteria.

If you need more time to fix an aspect of your marriage, then take more time. My friend, you and your spouse are supposed to live 'till death do you part', therefore you have literally a lifetime available for you to solve all your issues and cultivate a satisfying and fulfilling married life. Your marriage is like a baggage that you take around with when you are travelling. Sometimes, our bags are cluttered with things that we don't really need. Your marriage bag might be filled to the brim with resentment, jealousy, impatience, and other negative emotions that are weighing heavily on your relationship. The problem is no matter how much goodness you try to put in your marriage, if there is no space for it, then it still won't work. Therefore, the first step would be to remove the excess contents of your bag. And after that, you can replace it with the things that you really need – love, faithfulness, patience, kindness, and a lot of positive things.

4. Be disciplined in follow through

At the end of this chapter, there are reflection questions that you can use to have some form of healthy discussion with your spouse with regards to the concepts and principles that you have learned. I encourage you to take those questions seriously. Learning about the thoughts of your spouse will develop a deeper connection between the two of you. At the same time, you can also identify the possible loopholes that you need to address to make your marriage more vibrant and healthier. Also, there is a complimentary workbook that you can use in order to take the practical application of the concepts learned to the next level. The workbook consists of a more comprehensive list of thought-provoking questions and practical suggestions that you can implement to craft a more robust strategy to make your marriage work. So be sure to implement it as well.

Before We Begin

The principles and concepts that you will learn in this book are proven to help couples in cultivating a healthier and a more successful marriage. I believe that I have already established the fact that there is no perfect marriage, but regardless of this truism, I believe that you can work on towards having that ideal marriage. The key word there is the word *'work.'* Marriage is work – in fact, it is hard work – and the only way to make it work is when both spouses are willing to work. Yes, it has always been the same from the time of the first couple in the Garden of Eden up to the newlyweds that just recently took their vows.

"A divorce-proof marriage is team work in action" Chindah Chindah

The *Twelve* are proven, they are timeless principles to have a successful marriage, but it will only prove its worth in your own relationship if you are willing to put in the hard work. Nicholas Sparks, in his novel *"The Notebook"* captures the essence of this concept, the protagonist Noah said, *"So it's not gonna be easy. It's going to be really hard; we're gonna have to work at this everyday, but I want to do that because I want you. I want you. I want all of you, forever, every day. You and me... everyday."*

INTRODUCTION

Are you ready to have a lasting, satisfying and fulfilling marriage? Then turn to the first chapter and let's get to work!

Chindah Chindah
www.chindahchindah.com
www.limitlesslifepro.com
England, United Kindom.

THE MARRIAGE MYTHS

CHAPTER 1

"I do not think you can name many great inventions that have been made by married men."

– Nikola Tesla

What does a great marriage look like?

When can you say that a couple is happily married?

What are the signs that a relationship will last?

These are valid questions. In fact, I believe that any sane person who wants to participate in marriage must ask these questions. However, what's bothering me is the plethora of possible answers to these inquiries. And I am bothered because we live at a time when most of the ideas and concepts of people about marriage are derived from fairy tales, Hollywood movies, and best-selling fictional novels about vampires and wolves.

Due to the widely accepted pattern and rise of divorce statistics among many couples, I decided to study great marriages and failed marriage alike coupled with my personal experiences. My findings convinced me that, a true and a happy marriage is possible and within reach. However, this is dependent on the couple's knowledge of the principles and secrets of a successful marriage.

For instance, an individual might view marriage as something perfect, it's a union that is built to last and can go against all odds. Also, some understand that happily married couples are those couples who never argue and always agree about everything. Happily married couples always think the same about anything, they adapt to one another, and they lovingly adhere to each other's opinions. They are the perfect match,and because of these *deep* connection that binds them, their relationship is being strengthened and for sure, it will last. Or is it? Do these things really reflect the kind of marriage that most successful couples have?

In this chapter, I will like to address the most common myths and misconceptions about marriage. If we are to build the right foundation, then we need to tear down the pretentious and false information that we have when it comes to marital relationships. I challenge you to have an open mind as we discuss each myth and evaluate your own perception if you have built your notions of marriage on views. I guarantee that after reading through this whole chapter, you would have a renewed perspective on marriage and that newly formed paradigm will help you to lay the necessary foundation for the *Twelve* criteria that we will discuss in the succeeding chapters.

The 10 Myths about Marriage

"Be careful of what you believe about your marriage, because what you believe can actually happen and affect your marriage eventually" Chindah Chindah

What comes to your mind when you hear the word *'myth'?* For me, the first thing that comes to my mind is Hercules and the gods of Olympus. As a child, Greek mythology provided me with wonderful stories of gods, demi-gods, supernatural abilities, powers, and struggles. I marveled at the ability of Zeus to flash down lightning and the dreaded the power of Hades to bring people to the *Underworld.* I was amazed at the demi-god, Hercules and raised my fist for the god of war, Ares. However, as I grew older, I became aware that these characters are just work of fictions. They portray wonderful stories, but in the end, they are just a figment of someone's imagination.

Here's the tricky part. Imagine what will happen if I will live my adult life believing without a shadow of a doubt the myths that I watched when I was just a child. Think about the silliness of seeing normal people as demi-gods or monsters in disguise. It looks incredulous, don't you think? Perhaps, it's downright stupid. But what if the same scenario played out in your marriage? You gave your vow to your spouse while expecting a lot of myths about life in matrimony. Then, while in the middle of it all, you will just find yourself asking questions and your inner dialogue goes, *"Well, this is not what I expected."*

One of the most frustrating and embarrassing part of being married is to build it while having myths and misconceptions as your foundation. There is nothing more disappointing than finding out that you have constructed your most important relationship on the imaginary bricks and mortars of popular but make-believe love story. To avoid that, let me educate you on the most common myths and misconceptions about marriage.

Myth #1 Marriage is Supposed to Be Easy

According to research and studies, the intoxicating emotions and feelings of being in-love are high for couples who are just beginning in the relationship. However, the scientists have identified that the romantic emotions that new couples feel for each other wear off after 12 months. During the initial stage of intoxication, where couples might feel palpitation, sweaty palms, and butterflies-in-the-stomach, they might also feel that they can overcome anything. The flaws of each individual partner are easily overlooked while the admirable qualities are being exaggerated.

The problem arises when the couple assumes that the strong emotional attachment will stay forever and they decide to marry while they are in the intensity of their feelings for one another. However, once the romantic intoxication wears off, each individual will face the brutal fact that the person they chose to marry is not the person that they expected them to be. The imperfections will surface, the difficulty of living with another equally independent individual will be highlighted, and the burden of responsibility of building a family and providing for it will now come to light. And then, it will hit you. With the growing disappointments, unmet expectation, and increasing load of marital obligation, divorce becomes a possibility. Marriage is not easy.

Let's face it. All of these painful experiences can be avoided if only both persons are aware of what marriage truly entails. If each spouse was able to properly contemplate and consider all the changes that the wedding will bring to their lives – if each spouse knows that marriage is not easy – then they can also prepare properly to what lies ahead. It doesn't mean that there will be no problem when the couples are adequately equipped, though. But they will have the necessary tools to weather any storm that comes in their relationship.

So forget the notion that your childhood fairy tale told you that the prince and the damsel who just know each other for two days will just ride towards the sunset and will live happily ever after – just like that. 'Happily ever after' is not just about the fancy emotions of love, it involves commitment, passion, faithfulness, patience, attention and connection - indeed, great marriages are a result of hard work.

Myth #2 Marriage Will Bring You Closer Together – Automatically

A lot of people think that the best way for them to get closer together is to marry. In fact, in a survey conducted by Pew Research Center, one of the top 3 reasons why couples choose to marry is because of companionship. People have this innate desire to be with someone else. Most of us dream of marrying one day and spending the rest of our lives with someone else. When we think we found the right person, we do our best to spend more time with them. Late night talk on the phone, constant communication through social media, and as if the couples can't get enough of each other, they build a schedule to make sure that they spend time together.

Having this new person in your life brings a lot of mystery. You want to know him more and you want to get intimately deeper in your knowledge about your partner. Indeed, one of the greatest needs of man is to be known and to be loved. As author Donald Miller once said, *"I have sometimes wondered if the greatest desire of man is to be known and loved anyway."* And who wouldn't want it? Who wouldn't want to have a person beside her who shows a genuine interest in knowing her? Who wouldn't want to have someone who is ready to accept him, in spite of his shortcomings and flaws and love him, anyway?

It is indeed a great blessing and for us to keep it, the most logical way is to marry the person and talk all night until the rooster crows. In marriage, two separate individuals share a profound connection with each other and this connection can truly give them a sense of intimacy and togetherness – it is companionship at its finest. However, what will you do if you feel that all you need to learn from the other person is already out in the open? What will you do when the mystery is gone because you thought that you have revealed everything that is there to reveal to each other? And what about the imperfections of your spouse that is now glaring at you?

When we believe that marriage will automatically bring us closer together, then we are setting ourselves for great disappointments. Just like the other aspects of our relationships, connection and intimacy don't happen on its own. If you think that you have learned everything that you need to learn about your spouse then you are connecting with her in a wrong way. Humans are complex beings; they can't be put in a box to the effect that you tell yourself that you know everything about the person. In fact, thinking in this manner just shows the shallowness of the way you think.

If you want to learn more about a person, then talk with her; don't marry her just for the sake of being close to her. Do not allow your selfishness to reign and use marriage to satisfy your desire of having her around, because marriage can't guarantee that it will bring you closer automatically. Connecting with each other doesn't end with the wedding day. In fact, it's just the beginning of a greater need to develop intimacy and cultivate your relationship.

Myth #3 Marriage Will Always Make Things Better for Couples

Are you so madly in love right now with your partner? Then, marriage will further intensify that love between the two of you.

Are you faithfully committed to each other right now? Then, marriage will just strengthen the bond all the more to help you loyally stay in each other's arms. Are you extraordinarily generous to your partner, or perhaps you are wonderfully patient with him? Then, it's time to marry, because it will just increase your level of generosity with one another and make you more patiently loving towards him. That is what marriage does for your relationship!

Well, sorry, I want to politely ask you to disregard that previous paragraph because these are all lies. Those ambitious things about marriage can be considered as myths. In a study conducted by the National Opinion Research Center at the University of Chicago, they found out that the rate of *"happy couples"* is declining rapidly. In 2014, only 60% of surveyed individuals have reported that they are very happy in their married life. This rate is down from 65% with the survey conducted in 2012. Chris Donaghue, Ph. D., an author and a sex therapist cited various reasons for this phenomenon including waning sex lives, increasing desire for individualism, and the growing dependence of people to social media. So much of marriage making things better, right?

If the result of this survey will be our basis for debunking this myth, then we have ample evidence to say that the happiness and satisfaction that couples feel with regards to their relationship is not just being improved by marriage. That is to say that marital commitment to a person does not guarantee that everything will just magically stay better. In fact, the opposite might be true. Let me rephrase that first paragraph with the real possibilities that marriage can do to your relationship.

Are you so madly in love right now with your partner? Then beware, marriage might reveal to you the true character of the person that you love and it might affect the love that you have for him when you learn that he picks his nose and eat what he gets. Are you faithfully committed to one another right now? Then, marriage will test that commitment especially when you don't have any other option but to stay with that person for the rest of your life. Are you extraordinarily generous to your partner, or perhaps you are wonderfully patient with him? Then, think carefully before you marry, because it might hurt you when you are just the only person giving in the relationship. Also, just so you know, your person has an annoying habit that he carefully conceals so you will stay with him. That is what marriage does for your relationship!

The truth is marriage is like a blank canvass. The picture that will appear on it will be based on the colors of paint you use and the strokes of the brush that you make. A great picture of marriage won't happen magically on its own. Depending on the level of your connection with one another, the allowance that you gave for each other's shortcomings and your dedication to love each other in spite of all the things that happen will determine whether things will be better for you after marriage or it will just turn for the worst.

Myth #4 Married Couples Will Always Feel In love

According to a study conducted by Pew Research Center, 88% of Americans surveyed said that the love for each other is a very important reason to get married. Besides, if you have a choice, why will you opt to marry a person you don't really love? Love is one of the primary motivations for a couple to choose to tie the knot and spend the rest of their lives with another individual. But what if the love is gone? What if the emotional attachment and romantic feelings that they feel for each other slowly vanish? Does it mean that the couple have now sufficient ground to call their marriage quits?

It has already been ascertained and agreed by most psychologists and scientists that the intoxicating feeling in love doesn't really last for long. Whether it's 12 months, 24 months or 36 months, the general consensus of scientists is that the feelings of being mad and crazy in love with another person will eventually deplete. The chemicals at work in our brain – responsible for activating the same areas of our brain that could equally be activated by cocaine – will sooner or later settle down. From the intense romantic love, the emotions will turn into a tamer version which researchers want to call companionate love.

So, if you will ask me if married couples will always feel that highly intense romantic love like at the beginning of their relationship, then we have just debunked that myth using the results of research and studies of well-informed scientists. But then, ask me if married couples can stay in love after so many years, then I can give you a resounding, *"Yes, they can!"*

Whether we admit it or not, there are couples out there who have been married for so many years now, but still remain in love with each other. In fact, in a study conducted in 2012, published in the journal of *Social Psychological and Personality Science,* of couples who have been married for a decade, the researchers found out that 40% of the partners said that they were *"very intensely in love."* In the same study, they found out that couples who were married for 30 years or more, 40% of women and 35% of men said that they are very intensely in love with their partners.

At this point, I believe that an important distinction must be made. It seems that when it comes to marriage and romantic relationships, there are two kinds of love that we can observe. First is the kind of love that new couples feel for each other. It's the type of love that is highly intense, emotional and addictive. However, in spite of its intensity, this kind of love is temporary. After a couple of years in the relationship, the crazy love will be replaced by a more pacified version. This kind of love, if nourished, can help the couple stay intensely in love with each other despite the long time that has passed.

The addictive love won't stay for ever, therefore, it's a myth to think that married couples will always feel this level of love for each other. However, the lasting kind of love is possible, therefore, couples can still stay in love even after the initial stage of their relationship.

Myth #5 Getting Married Will Provide a Deeper Sense of Trust and Security

Some couple decide to get married for the sheer reason that they want to take advantage of the security that it offers. For them, having a paper that confers authorisation on he union and the ring that symbolises it increase the security of the relationship in a more significant way compared to just words of affection and acts of love. Also, these couples who believe in this principle see marriage as a way to establish trust between the spouses. If you are married to a person, you should now tell each other everything, right?

However, in a study conducted by Dr. Bella DePaulo which aims to assess the facts surrounding *lies* that an individual uses every day, Dr. DePaulo found out that couples are regularly deceiving each other. In fact, married couples are said to lie to each other once in every 10 interactions. Also, John Gottman also conducted a study on focus groups of couple and found out that trust and betrayal were the most important issues that plague the relationships of spouses.

How can an individual trust a person who regularly lies to her? In the same way, how can a couple have complete security from one another if deception – whether big or small – is becoming a daily part of their lives? Looking at the current perspective of people with regards to marriage, it can also be said that complete or even near-complete security of relationship is just an illusion. This is due to the reason that divorce is now a common occurrence for married couples in the society.

If there is one thing that marriage does when it comes to trust and security issues between the partners, it is to challenge it all the more. That is not to say that there could be no adequate trust and security in a marital relationship because those two things are essential foundations of a healthy marriage. What we can conclude is that just like the other aspects of marriage, trust and security don't just magically improve just because two persons get married. Deepening the sense of trust and security in the relationship can only be achieved if both spouses will uphold their integrity to each other and open the lines of communication which allows complete transparency between them.

Myth #6 Differences Will Ruin Your Marriage

We have this notion when it comes to romantic relationships that opposite attracts each other, just like two magnets with opposite poles. However, when it comes to marriage, most people think that these differences must be eliminated in order to avoid all kinds of disagreements and heated arguments. Well, it's true that some of the arguments and fights of couples arise as a result of their differences.

The husband might prefer to eat spaghetti tonight, but the wife is craving to eat soup for dinner. Who will give way? Or perhaps one of the spouses wants to watch an action movie while the other desires to see a romantic flick. These are petty issues but can still spark arguments between couples. And what about the more serious aspects of their relationship such as whether they should buy a new car, the way of disciplining their children, or the faith that the spouses should adhere to? Can these differences really cause damage and ruin the relationship of married couples?

You need to understand that each person is unique. Every individual has his own set of values, principles, and paradigms about life. He has also his own personality, character, habits and set way of thinking with regards to the people, things, and circumstances around him. And the truth is that some of these things cannot really be changed. For instance, the temperament of a person stays with him until his death. According to psychologists, there are four major temperaments that a person could have – Choleric, Melancholic, Phlegmatic, and Sanguine. An individual can have two major temperaments that he will display throughout his life.

Now, think about it, what if a Sanguine – who is typically an extrovert, loud, and confident person – marries a Melancholic, who is normally an introvert, silent and analytical person. As you can see, their temperaments are totally opposite and it is a perfect example of a glaring difference. If they marry and their desire is to stay with each other for the rest of their lives, does it mean that their marriage is inevitably heading for ruin? Hardly. Though their differing temperaments might cause some frictions in the relationship, having this kind of differences is not enough reason to say that they are doomed to divorce.

Marriage counselor, Robert C. Dodds said, *"The goal in marriage is not to think alike but to think together."* In short, differences between the spouses will always be present and there are aspects of a person's internal structure that can never be changed. So instead of trying to mould each other into a completely different person to avoid disagreements, the spouses must consider thinking together, feeling together, discussing together, and respecting each other's differences whenever it is appropriate. That is not to say that you will relate to your partner relationship in complacency by giving excuses like, *"That is just the way I am."*

Character must always be developed and cultivated. The character of patience, kindness, perseverance, and forgiveness must be imbued in the relationship. Character flaws must not be tolerated and left as is, rather the couple must work together to help each other develop a character that will make the relationship stronger and more satisfying for each other. On the other hand, personality differences, which are inborn, genetically inherited and God-given must be understood and celebrated.

Myth #7 Happily Married Couples Never Argue

This myth is also connected to the previous myth that differences ruin the marriage. As I have mentioned in the previous section, differences between couples are inevitable. No matter how hard you try to mould each other's personality to be exactly the same with each other, this feat is just impossible. With the differences in various aspects of each spouse's personality, arguments and heated discussions are always waiting to happen.

Arguments are a normal part of any relationship. In fact, in a research carried out by Esure, they discovered that couples fight on an average of 2,455 times a year. That seems a lot for couples, but it proves that arguing is indeed a normal component of any relationship. In another research done in India by a relationship site Shaadi.com in partnership with a research agency, IMRB, shows that 44% of married couples surveyed say that they believe that arguing regularly can keep the lines of communication open and strengthen the relationship between them. Recent studies also show that one of the leading symptoms of impending divorce for married couples is not the fact that they argue regularly, but rather the way they handle their arguments.

In a 14-year study conducted on 79 couples by John Gottman, a Psychology Professor at the University of Washington together with the Psychologist Robert Levenson of the University of California at Berkeley, they found out that those couples who argue but openly communicate and discuss the problem right after it happened stayed together while those couples who chose to wait and brush over the arguments were more likely to divorce. Also, spouses who disregard their partner's opinion in the middle of arguments end up in separation while those who waited patiently for their spouse to explain their sides and listen to each other's explanation have ended up with a stronger relationship.

Arguments and disagreements are normal between two unique and different individuals who are seeing things differently and married couples are the perfect examples of this. Based on the result of these studies, we can conclude that a fight doesn't necessarily have to be destructive for each other in the relationship. By using particular techniques of listening and understanding each other and extending respect for each other's opinions, arguments and fights can contribute to make the relationship stronger.

Myth #8 Your Spouse is Responsible for Your Wholeness

One of the most romantic lines that can be uttered by a person to their partner is this: *"You complete me."* Indeed, it is romantic. However, some people take it a notch higher by assuming that their partners are now responsible for their wholeness. That is to say that without their partners, they are not a whole person. As if not having the companionship and affection of their spouse will leave them incomplete.

If this is true, then every marriage is headed for divorce! Why? Because every person has his own imperfections and flaws. You can't expect your spouse to always be at 100%. The times when you will be both out of sync are inevitable no matter how hard you try to hold the relationship. And if problems and issues surface in your relationship, it will leave you devastated because your spouse and your relationship are the things that completes you.

Don't get me wrong; I believe that every couple must do their best to make each other happy and satisfied in their relationship. That is one of the most important aspects of their partnership. However, to put the burden of your own happiness on the shoulder of your spouse is too much to carry. It will weigh down on your partner and at the same time leave you disappointed.

I remember the story of John Maxwell and his wife Margaret Maxwell. In one of the lunch sessions, a lady politely asked Mrs. Maxwell whether her husband, John, is a good husband and if he makes her happy. Mrs. Maxwell smiled and answered the question quite frankly. She said, *"John is a good husband, but he doesn't make me happy."* A confused look appeared on the faces of people around the room, but before they come up with their own opinions, Mrs. Maxwell continued, *"He doesn't make me happy because I learned that I am responsible for my own happiness. My happiness doesn't depend on whether my husband will do good things for me. My happiness depends on my choice to be happy whatever the circumstances are."*

Isn't that true? Think of those times that you are in a bad mood but your partner noticed and does his best to make you happy. But you just don't want to be happy, that's why no matter what effort he exerts in making you smile, you just won't smile. Why? Because your happiness depends on your personal choice. Couples may always give comfort and encouragement to each other, but they still need to understand that they are responsible for their own happiness and feelings of wholeness.

Myth #9 Having Kids Will Improve Your Marriage

Most people, in one way or another, dreamt of building a loving family. The husband and wife loves each other unconditionally and find deep satisfaction in their relationship. And in order to further increase the intensity of love and fulfillment in the union, married couples should have children. The emotional satisfaction that a husband and a mother can feel once they have a baby should be the goal of every couple who wants to improve their marriage. Right? Wrong.

For 30 years, researchers have tried to find out the effects of having children in a marital relationship and the results of the study might surprise you. One of the major findings of the study is that having children doesn't really improve the relationship of spouses; in fact, it actually deteriorates because of it. Comparing couples with and without children, the researchers found out that the rate of decline in marital satisfaction is higher for those who have kids compared to childless couples. Not to mention that in those circumstances where the pregnancy is unplanned, the rate of decline is even higher.

These fundamental shifts in the dynamics of relationship between husband and wife are due to the fact that having a baby in the household is indeed a life altering experience. Priorities will be changed and the way that the couple interact with each other changes too. These changes are to facilitate the nurturing and caring for the new baby in the house. And if the spouses are not prepared to handle this kind of situation, their marriage could hit a wrong turn on the road.

However, it is also important to note that as the decline in marital satisfaction grows, the possibility of having a divorce also increases. This phenomenon gives the impression that both spouses are taking responsibility for the child and also willing to take on the burden of raising it. Indeed, having an additional member of the family can bring tremendous stress to the couple, but just like every problem, it can be weathered. According to Pamela Jordan, Ph. D., *"What's absolutely essential is two partners make a decision together to have a child."*

Myth #10 Cohabiting Before Marriage Will Ensure Its Success

We are living at a time where a lot of marriages are crumbling while divorce is gaining more and more popularity between couples around the world. Individuals are being hurt emotionally and children's hearts are being scarred permanently. Millions of pounds are being spent in lawsuits, court hearings and legal fees, while the emotional and psychological stress of breaking free from marriage cannot be neglected. This is the reality that we are living with right now and married couples are always in a constant risk of separation.

Divorce is indeed destructive in so many ways and perhaps that is the reason why a lot of people have tried to find a way to counter it. They came up with a great solution – cohabitation. And on the surface, they are winning it. The rate of divorce has been declining while the numbers of couples who are cohabiting are also rapidly rising. Now, can we conclude that cohabiting is the answer to ensure that marriage will be a success? Hardly.

In a study conducted by the Centre for Family Demographic Research of the Sociology Department at Bowling Green State University, they found out a lot of insightful facts about the concept of cohabitation and how it affects marriage, children, and relationship stability. Researchers studied a group of 707 women who cohabited in 1980s and 772 women who engaged in cohabitation in the late 2000s. They found out that cohabitation is indeed short-lived with half of the observed cohabitations dissolving within two years. As for the more stable cohabitations in the modern time, the researchers attributed it to the decline in marrying couples over the years.

But to answer the myth, the study also concluded that couples who live together in our modern days are less likely to get married in the near future. And if they will ultimately end up in marriage, about 20% of those cohabiting couples will still end up in divorce. In short, if a couple will choose to cohabit, there are three things that are most likely to happen. First, they will break up the relationship after some time; second, they will get married; third, they will still end up divorcing. Thus, debunking the myth that cohabitating ensures the success of a marriage.

Myths Are So Outdated

All of us want to have a lasting and satisfying marital relationship with the person that we love. A significant number of research and studies agree with the basic fact that marriage can bring tremendous benefits in health and emotional well-being of a person. However, a couple can only maximise those benefits if they will handle their marital relationship in the right way. And the best way to do that is to start debunking the old myths and misconceptions that they have about marriage and replacing it with sound principles and notions that can carry them towards a loving and committed relationship that is truly satisfying. Marriage is not dead. It is certainly alive. And its blessings and satisfactions are just waiting to be released on those persons who would actually take the challenge to understand it as it really is.

"You must be accountable and responsible for all that happens in your marriage for it to work" Chindah Chindah

Reflection Questions:

This portion of each chapter aims to help you and your spouse to properly evaluate the principles and concepts that you have learned. Try to answer truthfully all the questions. Discuss it with each other so you can gain a greater insight when it comes to your partner's ideas and personal thoughts. It will also be helpful if you can share your answers with another couple who might be delighted to go in the journey with you.

1. I copied the questions in the beginning of this chapter and put it here. Try to answer each question to the best of your ability, noting any significant differences between each response from both of you.

   What does a great marriage look like?

   When can you say that a couple is happily married?

   What are the signs that a relationship will last?

   _____

   _____

   _____

2. Going back to the *Top 10 Most Common Myths about Marriage*, what are the myths that you accepted as truth with regards to your perception of marital relationship? Can you identify the particular reasons why you end up believing these myths in the first place? Do you believe that all the 10 principles listed are myths? Why or why not?

   - **Myth #1** *Marriage is Supposed to Be Easy*
   - **Myth #2** *Marriage Will Bring Your Closer Together – Automatically*
   - **Myth #3** *Marriage Will Always Make Things Better for Couples*
   - **Myth #4** *Married Couples Will Always Feel In love*

- **Myth #5** *Getting Married Will Provide a Deeper Sense of Trust and Security*
- **Myth #6** *Differences Will Ruin Your Marriage*
- **Myth #7** *Happily Married Couples Never Argue*
- **Myth #8** *Your Spouse is Responsible for Your Wholeness*
- **Myth #9** *Having Kids Will Improve Your Marriage*
- **Myth #10** *Cohabiting Before Marriage Will Ensure Its Success*

_____

_____

_____

3. In relation to the myths and misconceptions that you believed about marriage, what are the steps that you are going to take in order to correct your perception about it? Also, how can your spouse help you move forward and take a significant step towards having the right perspective about marriage?

_____

_____

DYNAMICS OF DIFFERENCES

CHAPTER 2

*"A fruit salad is delicious precisely because
each fruit maintains its own flavor."*

– Sean Covey

We all accept the fact that each person is created unique. That is what our DNA tells us. Each person has his own genetic makeup and internal wirings. Every individual has his own unique set of personality, character, experience and paradigms in life. And this is true even in identical twins. Every person on the face of this planet is unique and teaming them up together with other people will bring all sorts of differences on the table. The differences are further highlighted when several factors come into play such as gender, age, nationality, culture, language and countless other things.

Now, try to picture out this scenario in the setup of marriage. Two unique individuals with several differences will try to live together in one house for the rest of their lives. The longer they stay together, the greater the sense of familiarity with one another will dawn on them and for the first time, they will see each other in a different light – warts and all. With the discovery of the flaws of his spouse, as well as the incompatibility between them, a nudging question might come up to both of them: *"Who is this person that I married?"* And the marital relationship will be more complicated from there.

That is what this chapter is all about. Since our differences are fundamental aspects of our individual personality and can either strengthen the relationship or spell disaster, a comprehensive discussion about it must be done. First, we focus on the basic differences between a man and a woman. How are we different biologically, psychologically or emotionally? And how does it affect the dynamics of our interaction inside the marital relationship? Second, we will address these differences head on by building the accurate mindset and principles of how we should see our differences. And lastly, we will discuss the correct way of dealing with differences inside the marriage and how we can leverage on it to make our marriage stronger and more fulfilling.

"The differences that exist between each spouse in a marriage union is not a threat to the relationship, but a blessing if both spouse understands this simple truth" Chindah Chindah

The Fundamental Differences of Man & Woman

Two persons might be born on the same day, attend the same school, and work in the same company but the other person makes two times more compared to the other. In the same way, a boy and a girl might have the same birthday, the same nationality, the same preference when it comes to food, music and the clothes they wear, graduated in the same year from the same university, in the same course and work on the same job, to the same boss, and with the same starting compensation package yet be worlds apart when it comes to their personality. In fact, I would like it to take it farther by saying that if their only difference is their gender, then the difference can still be worlds apart. Why? Because man and woman are differently wired. From the way their body react to stimuli, the way they think and see the world, as well as the way they feel about circumstances, men and women tend to show little similarities.

The difference between man and woman is no ground for disagreement. Just look at the reproductive organs of the two sexes and you can immediately see the difference. However, for the purposes of having a comprehensive understanding of the contrasting qualities between the two genders, let us further analyse the facts that science has given us so far.

WHAT CAN I DO TO MAKE MY MARRIAGE WORK?

1. Biological Differences

One of the major differences between a man and a woman when it comes to biological makeup is their ability to be fertile. Men can be fertile from puberty to almost up to 100 years old, though admittedly, the quality of the sperm and the ability of the male decreases as he becomes older and older. On the other hand, women can be fertile for about 12 hours each month and will stop at about age fifty when they undergo menopause. In addition to their ability to reproduce, men and women are also significantly different when it comes to` the chemicals – androgens and estrogens – that influenced the physical features of each gender. These differences are more evident when an individual transitions to puberty.

I stumbled across this list of 25 biological differences between man and woman that is both fun to learn and at the same revealing of how different we really are from one another. Source: list25.com

1. *Male newborn babies are more likely to have defects compared to their female counterparts. This is because of the presence of an extra copy of X chromosome for female babies whenever they have a defect.*

2. *In general, veins of male tend to be larger than female's.*

3. *Males are 4 times more likely to be autistic than females.*

4. *Males' foreheads tend to be more sloped while female foreheads tend to be more vertical.*

5. *The bodies of male have the capacity to deposit fats between organs. On the other hand, female bodies placed the fat as a ring around the abdomen. For this reason, you can easily tell someone's gender using an MRI, and it also makes liposuction easier for females.*

6. *Compared to their female counterparts, on average, males tend to have longer eyelashes. This might be contrary to popular belief of most people.*

7. *When it comes to the structure of fingers, the first finger of a male's hand is usually shorter than the third. On the other*

hand, females' hands typically have longer first finger compared to the third.

8. *Only females can pass mitochondrial diseases on to their offspring.*

9. *Males have a higher tendency to stutter compared to females. The ratio is about 3 to ??times.*

10. *Both sexes have the tendency to lose hearing on either end of the spectrum. However, males tend to lose their hearing on high pitched sounds, while females tend to lose their hearing onlow pitched sounds.*

11. *Compared to their male counterparts, females are considerably better in distinguishing shades of different colors.*

12. *Blood flow is more evenly distributed in the male body. In females it is concentrated around core organs and the pelvic region.*

13. *When it comes to genes, about 1,000 genes are said to be different between males and females with regards to the liver. For this reason, processing of chemicals that enters the body are being done at different rates between sexes.*

14. *Females tend to have a broader face than males.*

15. *The external occipital protuberance (the bump on the back of your skull) is bigger in males than in females.*

16. *The female jaw bone is lighter than themale jaw bone.*

17. *According to some studies, males tend to have more standard deviation when it comes to IQ.*

18. *Women tend to gather a greater proportion of their energy from aerobic respiration; men tend to spend more time in anaerobic respiration, relatively speaking.*

19. *The top edge of the eye socket is much sharper in females than in males.*

20. *Females have better peripheral vision than males, while males are typically better at scanning. This is thought to have evolutionary origins (hunters vs gatherers).*

21. *During heart attacks, males experience the "classic" symptoms*

like chest and jaw pain, while for females the symptoms can be quite diverse. In fact, it can often be confused for heart burn.

22. *Females' blood contains more water and about 20% less red cells.*

23. *Although female brains are better at many other tasks, male brains are geared towards giving them better spacial cognition.*

24. *Females tend to get motion sickness more easily, especially if they are pregnant.*

25. *Males die more from almost every disease except breast cancer, female reproduction disorders, and benign tumors.*

Indeed, when it comes to biological and physiological features, males and females have a lot of notable differences. In most cases, these particular set of differences between genders help them to define their roles in the household. For instance, when it comes to heavy lifting, a man is expected to do it for his woman because males are more physically equipped to do it.

2. Psychological Differences

Scientists have discovered that there are approximately 100 differences in the brain of males and females that are primarily determined by their gender. When studying the distinguishers between the sexes, the scientists are generally dividing their research into four major categories, namely: *processing, chemistry, structure and activity.* These four major areas of brain and neurological functions can provide useful insights when it comes to the behavior of men and women.

Processing

This area of the brain study focuses on how an individual uses his brain to process information and deal with circumstances around him. Scientists found out that male brains uses nearly seven times more gray matter when it comes to their activities while female brain uses approximately ten times more white matter.

The gray matter of the brain represents those areas that are localised. It pertains to information and action processing centres located in specific areas of the brain. It means that when an individual utilise these gray matters, they tend to be more focused and concentrated in what they do – a classic example of having a tunnel vision. That is the reason why a man who is engaged in a task is typically absorbed in what he does, whether it's working on an important project or concentrating on a game. During this period, a man might not demonstrate sensitivity and awareness to other people and his surroundings.

The white matter, on the other hand, pertains to those areas of the brain that connects the gray matters with other processing centers. Because of these connections, a person can easily switch from one task to another. That is why most females can easily transition between different activities than males do. Unlike their male counterparts, females can quickly get out of a task and do other things as the need arises. The difference in the utilization of gray and white matters of the brain might explain the reason why women are considered great in multitasking while men excel in being highly focused and concentrated.

Chemistry

Both male's and female's bodies utilise varying degrees of neurochemicals inside their bodies which governs the various specific body-brain activities. However, the level of neurochemicals being used differs between genders. Scientists have noted that females use more *serotonin* compared to males. This neurochemical is the one responsible in helping a person to sit still for an extended period – a disposition that is more noticeable in females. Another neurochemical that is more dominant in females is the *oxytocin,* which is also called the bonding-relationship chemical. The dominance of this neurochemical in females might explain why they tend to lean more on connecting and relating to other persons compared to their male counterparts. As for the males, scientists noted that they are more inclined to produce more testosterone which explains why men are more physically impulsive and aggressive when compared to women.

WHAT CAN I DO TO MAKE MY MARRIAGE WORK?

Structure

Differences between male and female were also noted in terms of specific parts of their brain structure, the way it is built, and also the size and mass of these parts. Females are noted to have larger hippocampus compared to males. The hippocampus is the human memory center that enables us to recall the things that happened in the past. In addition to having a bigger hippocampus, it was also discovered that females have a higher density of neural connections inside it which will heighten their ability to sense what is happening around them while giving the capacity to retain those information – an ability that is more notable for females compared to males.

In addition to this, the brains of female have verbal centers on both sides of the brain while males tend to have only verbal centers on the left hemisphere. The presence of verbal centers on both hemispheres for women enables them to use more words when communicating about almost everything. On the other hand, men tend to have fewer verbal centers in general, have lesser connectivity when it comes to the way they discuss things using words even when it is about memories or their feelings.

Activity

The blood flow and brain activity of males and females also differ from each other. The female brain is discovered to have a more natural flow of blood throughout the brain – the white matter processing – and also higher degree of concentrated blood flow in an area called *cingulate gyrus.* This is what helps females to reflect and remember emotional memories more compared to males. On the other hand, males tend to just reflect briefly on an emotional memory, analyse it for a short time and move on to the next task. Men have a lesser tendency to carefully analyse their emotions and do something that is totally unrelated to their feelings.

These four major categories and the examples cited are only but a few differences that could be noticed in psychological and neurological make up of males and females. However, having a proper understanding of how the brain works can indeed provide useful insights on specific behaviors of both sexes.

3. Emotional Differences

Another area where a large number of visible differences could be noticed is in the aspect of handling emotions. Based on general observation, most people say that women are more emotional compared to men. However, based on what we learned in the previous section, most of the responses of both genders can be traced back to the neurological make up of males and females. It's really about how the brain works which is proven by a recent large-scale study conducted by the University of Bagel.

The study involved 3,400 test participants and the researchers designed an experiment aimed at determining whether women perform better than men in memory tests by taking into account their ability to process emotional information. Images that show emotional content were rated by women as more emotionally stimulating than men, specifically in those pictures that display negative images. As for the neutral images, both genders responded the same. After the exposure to all images, the participants have undergone a memory test and during this test, the researchers have noted that the females were able to considerably recall more images compared to males. The study's leader, Dr. Annette Milnik said, *"This would suggest that gender-dependent differences in emotional processing and memory are due to different mechanisms."*

Based on this recent study, we can conclude that the differences into emotional processing are primarily linked to memory and brain activity. Indeed, the study provides some clarifications on the dynamics of emotional variation between genders. However, I believe it will also be helpful to identify some major emotional differences between men and women as observed by psychologists in the actual setup of romantic relationships. Here are some of them:

- *Men desire to feel needed and respected while women need to feel appreciated and cherished.*

- *Men regularly need to have time alone, while most women*

regularly need someone to talk to.

- *Men want to feel accomplished, women want to feel worthy of love.*
- *Men process emotions by allowing space to think, women process emotions by talking about it.*

Learning about the neurological answers to the emotional processing of your spouse might be a challenging task. However, you can simplify the process by learning to observe some nonverbal hints and also having a general understanding of how males and females process their emotions. Trust me, it's worth the time and effort and might save you from a lot of needless pain.

Basic Principles about Differences in Marriage

One of the myths that we have discussed in the previous chapter is the myth that differences will ruin your marriage and we have argued that it is indeed a myth. However, I must admit that it is not completely a myth because it shows one side of the coin when it comes to the effect of difference of couples in physiological, psychological, and emotional makeup. Differences between the spouses can indeed ruin the marriage if those things are not be handled properly. But at the same time, the same differences between two individuals in a marital relationship could be used to strengthen their bond and connection. How is that possible?

As we all know, one of the primary ingredient needed to brew conflict is having some sort of differences. People who have differing opinions about politics or religion are ripe for having a heated argument. In the same way, couples who have different personalities, desires, and perspectives are always in danger of fighting over a lot of things. However, that is not the actual problem. Psychologist professor, John Gottman said, "*Most couples tend to equate a low level of conflict with happiness and believe the claim 'we never fight' is a sign of marital health. But I believe we grow in our relationship by reconciling our differences. That's how we become more loving people and truly experience the fruits of marriage.*"

Reconciling your differences is indeed a major factor in resolving any argument that might arise in the course of your relationship. Here are some things that you must understand in order to set the foundation for effective difference reconciliation.

1. Differences in Marriage is Inevitable

We have considerably established the fact that man and woman are created and wired differently in almost every aspect of their being. Therefore, arriving at the conclusion that we cannot avoid having differences in marital relationship are fairly logical and in fact, plainly common sense. Understanding this concept is crucial especially for those couples who are just starting in their marriage. There will always be things that they won't see similarly, responses from each other that they might consider an outlier in the norm, and countless details in their relationship that they will process differently.

Marrying another person doesn't mean that you need to conform yourself to what your partner is. In fact, marrying another person must evoke the willingness of each spouse to accept their differences and find some form of common ground in other aspects of their union. Differences in marriage is inevitable and the sooner you accept that, the earlier you can work together in building a marriage that founded on respect and acceptance.

2. Marriage Should Not Extinguish our Differences

The greatest risk when it comes to dealing with differences between spouses is the natural tendency to influence or much worse, to force the other person to change. Before entering the relationship, most people have a mental picture of the ideal person that they want to marry. However, because of the intoxicating emotions that the initial stage of love brings, they tend to gloss over the inconsistencies in the mental picture and the actual person of their beloved. But as we have discussed earlier that the emotional high of young love will eventually fade and couples will now see their partner without their rainbow colored glasses.

If one of the couple is dominant and still too idealistic, she might influence her partner to change and conform to the picture that she had in her mind before entering the relationship. Perhaps, she wants him to be more talkative, or maybe she likes her husband to be more outgoing and sociable. The problem is that attempts to change your partner will only cause friction and conflict between the two of you, especially if the aspects that you want to influence are those areas that can be considered as non-negotiable.

Healthy marriages thrive without the need of transforming a person to another that is completely not him. Couples need to learn that the goal of marriage is not to extinguish or eliminate the differences but rather to celebrate it, recognise your partner's uniqueness and utilise those differences to be more creative and to further build the foundation of marital relationship.

3. Acceptance and Disagreements

The concept of dealing with the differences between married couples will be discussed later in this chapter. For now, let me give you a brief summary of having the basic principles of acceptance and disagreements when it comes to this aspect of marital relationship. First, there are aspects of a person's design that he won't be able to change for you no matter how much he tries. In our career, there are times that we were made to do something that might feel awkward and uncomfortable. If this happens to you, chances are you had done something that was out of your genetic makeup or personality.

For instance, introversion will always stay with a person. No matter how hard a person tries to become an extrovert, if he is not really that kind of person, then eventually he will just go back to who he really is. This kind of things must be accepted when it comes to dealing with differences because you can't really change it and forcing your way of things will just hurt the relationship and may cause sharp disagreements between you and your spouse.

On the other hand, there are things that can still be changed and must be changed in order to make the relationship stronger. For instance, being constantly late in your dates might be taxing the emotional reserves of your partner because she feels that you don't really prioritize your time together. This harmful habit can be changed with a few tweaks in your scheduling and priority management. It might cause some disagreement between couples because of the tendency that this particular bad habit might persist, but it's something that can help both of you in your marriage.

Understanding these basic principles is fundamental in handling conflict that might arise because of differences between you and your spouse. Mastering the essence of these principles is indeed instrumental in a healthy resolution of conflicts. Go over once more on those three ideas and see how it can apply to your marriage.

Change It or Accept It?

Differences between spouses can come in all shapes and sizes. And across the wide variety of possible distinguishers are countless other details that might come into play inside the marital relationship. With all these possible differences between spouses, it is important to understand that there are just some things that should not be brought up, while there are other aspects that must be overhauled for the benefit of the relationship. The question now is this: *How do we know if something must be changed or accepted? To* answer that question we need to carefully identify the specific differences between individuals and subject it to the following test, which is represented by the flowchart below:

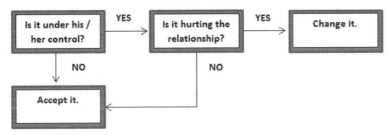

Well, of course, the actual dynamics of differences between married partners are more complicated than this simple flow chart, but we can still use it as a guide to consider if some aspects of the relationship or even the actual characteristics of an individual must be changed. Let us further elaborate on those questions and identify the major aspects that qualify in each category:

1. Differences That Are Not Under the Control of a Person

These are the things that an individual has no control over or can influence – in short, these are the things that he can't change no matter how much he likes to change it. They are just irreconcilable, something that should just be accepted. Here are some examples of differences under this category:

- *Nationality or place of birth*
- *In-laws*
- *Temperaments*
- *Past experiences*
- *Age*

Now, you might say, *"Some of these things are just common sense, isn't it?"* But let me tell you that there are still married couples who argue because of disagreements with the in-laws, the basic temperament of the husband or the wife, or those past relationships that have been over for almost five years. These things might result to some form of stress to the couples, but there are no other ways but to accept these things because they are not under the control of either of the spouses.

However, this should not be a reason for complacency inside the relationship. You cannot use your past experiences as an explanation for why you are behaving in a particular manner. In the same way, your temperament should not be used as an excuse why you are ignoring your spouse's needs. The truth that these things cannot be changed is not sufficient to warrant any form of complacency between the spouses. You might not be able to change your past, but you have all the power to change how you look at it. You won't be able to change your age, but you can work on your level of maturity.

2. Differences That Can Be Controlled But Not Hurt the Relationship

Some differences might be so glaring, but do not necessarily affect the relationship in a bad way. The couples could chose to work on changing them or they can agree to just leave them as they are. Either way, it won't significantly affect the relationship or even the spouse involved. Here are some examples of this kind of differences:

- *Preferred diet*
- *Way of unwinding from stress*
- *Political views (as long as you respect each other's opinion)*
- *Individual habits and routines*

Have you seen couples who are worlds' apart when it comes to their preferred diet? The guy wants to eat a lot of pizza, while the pretty lady prefers eating healthy foods such as salad and sugar-free drinks. There are also a lot of other couples who have diverging preference in their way to unwind from stress. Perhaps, the man wants to go outdoors and spend time with nature, while the woman is content with staying at home while watching some movies. Or you might also encounter a couple who support different Presidential candidates. They can argue passionately about why their candidate is the better person for the position without bordering disrespect for one another. And lastly, there are also a lot of spouses who possess different habits and routines.

These differences are relatively changeable depending on the individual and collective decisions of the partners. But it doesn't mean that it might affect the relationship in a negative way. Changing it or leaving it as it is will just have little to no effect on their condition as marital partners. In fact, the couple might just agree to respect their individual preferences and arrive at some form of compromise in establishing a middle ground.

3. Differences That Can Be Controlled and Hurts the Relationship

It is a proven and accepted fact that differences cannot be avoided in any kind of relationship due to the fact that we are individuals with unique genetic makeup, experiences, personalities and perspectives in life. Therefore, respecting the differences between spouses is one of the most important building blocks of a healthy relationship. Having the character to accept your spouse for who she is, indeed is an amazing gift that can be given by a spouse could give to his partner.

However, there are some kind of differences that could potentially hurt the relationship and hence, must be lovingly confronted and change. Changing these things does not mean that you don't want to accept the person, warts and all; it means that you are willing to adjust and do whatever is necessary in order to protect each other inside your marriage. Here are some examples of changes that must be addressed and subjected to change.

- *Values*
- *Attitudes*
- *Crucial Perspective About Family and Relationships*

Values pertain to an individual's concept and judgement of what's important in life. Attitudes are a set of settled way of thinking or feeling about something. It is usually manifested and displayed in the behaviour of the person who possesses it. Perspective can be loosely defined as a person's point of view. All these things were built and developed based on a number of factors such as upbringing, personal experiences, and outside influences.

Each person has their own set of values, attitudes, and perspectives. And when there are differences in any of those things, conflict might arise. For instance, a person who put so much value on his work and accomplishments and a lesser emphasis on family will likely go against a person who has contrary values. Imagine a couplewho have opposing values. The husband regards his career as more important and deserving more of his time. He therefore spends majority of his time at his work. his wife, on the other hand, sees her family as her top priority. Can you already see the potential conflict?

Let's try another example with regards to the differing attitudes of individuals. Think about an optimistic wife who always sees the positive in every situation. She believes in the potential of each person and all the great possibilities that could happen. On the other hand, her husband is a pessimist who always views the world with a sense of apprehension. Now, this could be an ordinary case of seeing the glass as half-empty or half-full. However, problems might arise if either of them goes to the extreme. For instance, the wife, being overly optimistic, enters every business deal that is presented to her without first conducting a thorough study.

In the same way, you can expect a lot of conflict when spouses have differing point of view when it comes to family and relationship. Think about a couple who both love their family very much. They believe in the importance of spending time with each other and cultivating the relationship by communicating regularly. However, their point of view diverges when it comes to disciplining their children. The husband, coming from a strict family, sees punishment as a necessary part of effective discipline while the wife, coming from a liberal family, believes that talking with the children is enough deterrent in avoiding future disobedience.

As you can see, values, attitudes, and perspectives run down deeply in the core of a person's being and changing or adjusting it is no easy task. Yet, being on the same page or at least having a clear understanding between couples when it comes to these areas is crucial in order to achieve a form of stability in the relationship. Thus, it should always be addressed and communicated between them.

Dealing with the Inevitability of Differences in Marriage

There could be a plethora of reasons why people are choosing to go into marriage. But if there is one thing that can be considered universal across all marriages – it is the inevitability of differences between spouses. Considering this fact, it is absolutely crucial for couples to have the necessary understanding and game plan to deal with this kind of issues inside their marital relationship. Yet, a lot of couples are addressing their dissimilarities in the wrong way. Some try to put their dissimilarities aside and agree on all things.

Others try their best to hide their differences based on the false notion that if you truly love your spouse, you will do anything to make her happy. And there are couples also who fear differences and are shock to realise that their spouse is so different from them.

If you want to enjoy your marital relationship and get the most out of your married life, then it is necessary to understand the right way to deal with differences. Here are some suggestions to help you.

1. Encourage and Celebrate Your Uniqueness

Looking at a different and more positive perspective, one of the greatest gifts of marriage is letting you to love someone who might be considerably different from who you are. With the diversity of the knowledge, experience, and point of views of your spouse, marriage is giving you a lot of opportunities to learn more other things. Perhaps your partner came from a different family background, now you have access to first-hand information on what it means to live without a mother or a father. Or maybe your spouse loves reading books, now you can also benefit from everything that he is learning by communicating about it.

What makes your husband unique? What are the qualities that make him different and special? What are the aspects of herself that you don't have, but you believe is admirable and desirable to learn? As long as your specific differences are not hurting your relationship and creating a rift between the two of you, then you can celebrate those things as beautiful and admirable qualities of each other. In fact, by having some sort of differences, you can have plenty of things to talk about and if you will just be open to hear what the other person has to say, then I can guarantee that you will learn a lot from each other.

Also, to encourage and to celebrate uniqueness means that you don't judge your spouse based on your differing traits, views, and opinions. It means that you won't judge your partner as lazy just because he doesn't prefer hiking up on mountains like your other friends. You won't also judge your wife just because she appreciates rap music while you appreciate ballads. A healthy marriage will celebrate uniqueness of each spouse, and if ever a particular difference might cause some form of argument, then both husband and wife must be quick to talk about it, try to understand each other, and create a middle ground if necessary.

2. Don't Conceal Your Differences

Have you watched the movie, *"Frozen?"* One of the famous lines that Elsa's father taught her is this: *Conceal. Don't feel.* Her father said it in relation to Elsa's supernatural power to control ice. However, this advice of her father didn't go so well and it left her more fearful and afraid of being herself. By concealing her true self and her uniqueness, she alienated her sister, creates a massive weather problem, and almost killed her sister, Anna. The point is, concealing does not do the trick when it comes to being different and unique. Can you imagine your spouse concealing her true self and not feeling what she would like to feel just to please you?

Your differences must be communicated to each other. Trying to mould yourself into a person that is not really you will just leave you frustrated and dissatisfied. However, this doesn't mean that you just assert everything about yourself. Remember that there are different kinds of differences and your response towards them will depend on whether they are hurting the relationship or not.

If you are putting so much value on your hobbies and recreational activities, and your values are making your spouse feel unloved and unappreciated, then it's not the time to assert your uniqueness. Concealing it won't also help. In that particular scenario, it would be greatly helpful if you and your spouse will be able to talk about it and try to adjust so that you can still enjoy your hobbies without neglecting your most important relationship.

3. Don't try to Change the Non-negotiable

It was already discussed that sometimes, the needs to adjust, change, and find a middle ground is the best way to address the differences. However, there are some aspects of a person's being that must be considered as non-negotiable. These aspects must be accepted as they are and changing them will just result to deeper wounds and bigger rifts in your marital relationship.

One great example of a non-negotiable aspect is the temperament of a person. If your spouse is an outgoing and outspoken Sanguine, don't try to change her into an introverted person like you. If she asserts her confidence and her capability to do things on her own, then don't fit her into an image of a damsel in distress. A person's temperament is at the core of her being and trying to morph it will just frustrate both spouses.

Another example of a non-negotiable difference is a person's love language. The Principle of Love Language was popularised by a marriage expert, Gary Chapman, in his book, *"The 5 Love Languages."* One of the main thesis of the book is that all persons have their own love language and for you to effectively communicate your love to them, you must speak their language. For instance, if your spouse feels deep affection from you when you spend time with her, then perhaps, she has the love language of quality time. The problem is that, you can't change it. No matter how much you try to express your love to your partner by giving gifts or massages, nothing will communicate stronger than spending quality time with her.

These non-negotiable must be acknowledged, understood, and communicated to each other. No crossing of boundaries; whatever temperament or love language a person has, it must be respected and celebrated accordingly. If your husband is an introvert, then lovingly accept him and admire him for his uniqueness. If you wife's love language is acts of service, then show your love for her by doing chores, lifting her bags or making her dinner occasionally.

Differences Can Be Healthy

Legendary basketball coach, John Wooden, said, *"Things turn out best for those who make the best out of the way things turn out."* The same can be said with marriage. The differences between spouses can be turned out for the best, as long as the couple will decide to communicate, understand, and celebrate their differences. Since no one can eliminate the dissimilarities between couples, all we need is to learn the proper way to address those aspects of the marital relationship. If the spouses can appropriately deal with their issues, then indeed, differences can be healthy. In fact, their differences and individual uniqueness can be used as building blocks to a more successful and happier marriage.

Reflection Questions:

This portion of each chapter aims to help you and your spouse to properly evaluate the principles and concepts that you have learned. Try to answer all the questions truthfully. Discuss it with your spouse so you can gain a greater insight when it comes to your partner's ideas and personal thoughts. It will also be helpful if you could share your answers with another couple who might be delighted to go in the journey with you.

1. Having differences between you and your spouse can never be avoided. There is a need to properly address those differences and it will start by identifying the specific differences that you have in terms of biological, psychological, and emotional aspects. If you have been in the relationship for a long time, then surely, you were able to spot some major differences in these three major categories. Try to give some examples, and be as specific as possible. Try to identify particular events or occurrences where each difference was highlighted.

_____

_____

2. Before reading this chapter, what were your perceptions when it comes to differences in marriage? Did you believe that in order for a marriage to be successful, differences must be eliminated? Now, based on what you have learned in this chapter, specifically the basic principles about differences, are there any notable changes in your perception? How does this change in your perception affect the way you treat the differences between you and your spouse? What specific actions will you take to display a more appropriate view of the those differences?

_____

_____

_____

3. There are different ways to deal with differences in marriage, and for some couples, they are doing it in the wrong way. How does your marriage fair when it comes to this aspect? How did you and your spouse address the differences that you have noticed in the past? What aspect of yourself have you concealed in order to avoid any argument with your partner? What specific things will you do to encourage and celebrate your individual uniqueness?

_____

_____

_____

4. We have discussed the importance of leaving the non-negotiable aspect of our individuality as it is. Try taking personal assessment examinations to identify the personality and temperament for the both of you. Also, read Dr. Chapman's book and take an assessment to identify your specific love language and that of your spouse. After identifying these things, think about the specific things you can implement in order to express more of your love for each other.

_____

_____

_____

FIRST CRITERION:
TRUE AND LASTING COMMITMENT

CHAPTER 3

*"Staying in love has nothing to do with luck
and everything to do with commitment."*

– Darlene Schacht

One of the most important ingredients of a healthy marriage is the unwavering love of the spouses to each other. However, while most people are emphasising the power of love to keep couples together, there is another essential foundation to make the marital relationship strong and steadfast. It is the foundation of *"commitment."* The sad thing is that in our world today, commitment is a word that is quickly losing its value and meaning. We commit ourselves to different meetings, yet we normally come late or even don't come at all. We commit our finances to a specific type of budget, but before we know it, we are buying things that we don't even need. And even in marriage, a lot of couples exchange vows of commitment to stay together, in sickness, and in health, 'till death do them part', yet a significant number of these couples will end up in divorce.

What is commitment, anyway? We use the word in different aspects of our lives, yet a lot of us have only a faint understanding of the true meaning that it should convey to us. And let me ask you this question, what comes to your mind when you hear the word *"commitment?"* For some, they think about their loan and the money that they committed to redeem it. Others will think of their physical workout and how they are committing themselves to a particular set of routine.

Still, regarding the word, I once came across a practical joke where a group of friends were talking about the most terrifying costume for Halloween. They wanted to wear something that will scare the living daylights out of everybody. A couple of horrifying characters like Dracula and the Swamp Monster were mentioned in the conversation until one of the boys said, *"I know what to wear in Halloween! It will absolutely scare everyone!"* The other people in the group curiously asked the guy, *"Is there even a costume that can frighten everybody?"* *"Yes,"* the guy said, *"it's Commitment!"* Indeed, a lot of people are scared of that word.

If commitment is indeed one of the most important building blocks of a successful marriage, then it is also essential for anyone who wants to enter into a marital relationship to gain an accurate understanding of what it is and its role in creating a strong marriage. In this chapter, we will define the word *"commitment"* and also elaborate on the different sources of an individual's commitment. We will discuss in detail the aspect of love and its importance in creating a lasting commitment between couples. I firmly believe that your level of commitment to a person will not exceed the level of your love for him, hence the importance of having a deeper understanding of the concept of love. Lastly, we will address the greatest destroyers of commitment and how to eliminate one of them. An extensive discussion about the concept of cohabitation will also be included in order to determine its dangerous effects on marriages around the world.

What Does It Mean to Commit?

"For your marriage to work, you must be all in at all times"
Chindah Chindah

The word *"Commitment"* was in popular use by people as early as the late 1500's or early 1600's and was originally used to denote the *"act of officially consigning to the custody of the state."* It already implies that the word describes the giving oneself to another through a promise, a pledge, or an engagement. Now, the dictionary defines the word as: *"the state or quality of being dedicated to a cause or activity"* and *"an engagement or obligation that restricts freedom of action."* In essence, committing yourself to a person, a cause, or a particular date and time means that you are giving a part of yourself to that thing. Perhaps, that is the reason why a lot of people today are afraid of commitment.

Commitment can come in different sizes and shapes because commitment might be a result of different sources. You can be committed to a specific organization and its cause. You might also be committed to a particular group of people. You can also be committed to a certain object, or a specific date, or even to an individual. And all of these commitments will cost you something. It might cost you your money, your time and even your life. For most people, it is hard to understand that they need to give themselves to only one thing while there are countless options available to them.

Why would you commit your financial resources to a specific house if there are thousands of equally good houses that you can choose from? Why would you dedicate your time to a single organisation if there are numerous activities that are vying for your limited hours everyday? Why would you commit yourself to a person – without an easy way out – if there are countless other persons who might be more beautiful, intelligent, or can provide an even perform better in bed? Let's face it: We don't want to be tied up with a single thing because we are afraid to make a mistake. Thus, commitment is being depreciated and its value is slowly being deteriorated.

Commitment in Marriage

A study was conducted by some UCLA psychologists that was centered on this question: *"What does being committed to your marriage really mean?"* The subjects of the study are 172 married couples who were analysed for over 11 years of marriage. The psychologists were able to find out that there are actually two kinds of commitment that could be seen in marital relationships. Benjamin Karney, a co-director of the study and a psychology professor said, *"When people say, 'I'm committed to my relationship,' they can mean two things. One thing they can mean is, 'I really like this relationship and want it to continue.'* This kind of commitment can be considered superficial because it is only based on the benefits that the individual is getting from the relationship. They are doing their best for it to continue because they are receiving some form of rewards from their spouse and from their marital relationship.

Another psychology professor who is a co-director of Relationship Institute that conducted the study, Thomas Bradbury, said, *"It's easy to be committed to your relationship when it's going well. As relationship changes, however, shouldn't you say at some point something like, 'I'm committed to this relationship, but it's not going very well – I need to have some resolve, make some sacrifices and take the steps I need to keep this relationship moving forward."* This kind of commitment is based on a person's resolve and decision. It doesn't matter whether things are going bad in the relationship; the important thing is that both persons are willing to make some sacrifice in order to help their relationship to continue.

These statements were proven by the study. Of the 172 married couples that took part in the study, about 78.5% were still married after 11 years while the remaining 21.5% were already divorced. What makes the difference? It was determined that those couples who stated that they are willing to make sacrifices for the sake of their relationship increased the likelihood that they will stay together, especially during those tumultuous times of their marriage. Karney answered the question about the meaning of commitment in marriage based on the results of the study. He said, *"It means do what it takes to make the relationship successful. That's what this research is saying. That's what commitment really means. In a long-term relationship, both parties cannot always get their way."*

The results of the study conducted by UCLA psychology professors are indeed revealing when it comes to the importance of commitment to sustain a marriage. If the resolve of the couple is not that strong and they can easily be swayed by problems and trials inside the relationship, then their weak commitment can be the cause of divorce. On the other hand, if the couple's decision is mature enough to accept the problems and strong enough to find solutions, then their marriage can stand the test of time. However, the saddening reality is that most people are choosing the easy way out or devising a way to outsmart the pillar of commitment by not entering into one. In light of everything that is happening now in the institution of marriage, we need an in-depth understanding of the value of commitment.

What is the Greatest Source of Commitment?

We have now established the importance of commitment in marriage. We were able to ascertain that the result of the marriage – whether it will last for a lifetime or will come crashing through a divorce – is determined largely by the degree of commitment that each spouse have for each other. Now the thing that we need to identify is the greatest source of that commitment.

You see, commitment can come from different sources. It can come from a person's desire to please his parents and the people around him so he won't subject himself to the shame of failure in divorce. Commitment can also result to a person's personal ambition. For instance, there are people who chose to get married to a person that they don't love but just for the sake of money. They might not love the person unconditionally, but their desire to get the best things out of this life motivates them to stay in the relationship. Still others base their commitment on their emotional security; they are committed to the person because there is no other alternative. Losing that person might leave them vulnerable and in extreme cases, might cause nervous breakdown or even death.

However, are these sources of commitment strong enough to make the relationship last? Think about the examples mentioned above. Basing your commitment on other people's approval will just make you frustrated over time, because you are an imperfect person and those people that you want to please are imperfect individuals. No matter what you do, people will always see flaws in you. And when you lose their approval, what will you do? End the relationship? Another is basing your commitment on money. Does it mean that when the money is gone, you will also lose your resolve to stay in the relationship? Lastly, if your commitment is based on your emotional security, then does that mean that when you become strengthened, you can just easily let go of the relationship because you no longer need it? These are real questions that demand honest answers, because somewhere, someone is going through this exact ordeals.

In spite of the negative sources of commitment, there is still what we can consider the greatest source of commitment. And that is a couple's love for each other. Love can be the difference maker. In fact, when you carefully examine it, people who are truly in love don't seek the approval of other people, thus the cliché saying, *"You and me, against the world."* Also, people who are in love naturally don't look at the financial capacity of a person. There are couples out there who are literally worlds apart when it comes to their wealth, but they still chose to love and commit to each other. Also, people who are truly in love can be secure enough with their partners. Considering all of these, then we can conclude that indeed, love is the greatest source of commitment.

The Different Types of Love

Commitment can either break the marriage or make it last. And the greatest source of that commitment is the love that each spouse has for their spouse. However, the problem is this: *A lot of us don't really have a clear idea of what true love is.* Let's face it, when talking about love, most people's knowledge about it came from fairy tales, romantic movies, books, or even other people's distorted perception of it. We use the word *"love"* in our everyday lives, but most of us don't really understand its true meaning. A person might say that he *loves* watching movies, but the same person might also say *"I love you"* to another. In fact you might say *"I love you"* to your spouse, to your parents, and to Hugh Jackman, while conveying three different meanings at the same time.

In order for us to understand the true meaning of love, we need to first identify it based on its rightful category. Yes, my friend, there are different categories of love. That will explain how you can say that you love your partner and you love eating salad without confusing what it really means. However, to easily facilitate the process of identifying the different types of love, we will use the translation of the word *"love"* based on its different shades of meanings as used by original ancient writers of the Bible. Here are the four different types of love:

1. Eros

Eros is one of Greco-Christian terms that are usually translated as the word *'love'* in the Bible. It commonly connotes the idea of sexual love and desire for another person or the feelings of being aroused that two people share when they become physically attracted for each other. In fact, *Eros* is the root of the English word, *Erotic,* which relates to being arouse in sexual desire or excitement. Thus, from these concepts, we can consider *Eros* as the romantic form of love bordering on sexual physical attraction to another person.

If we will relate it to what we have talked about in commitment, then *Eros* form of love will not be enough to build a lasting commitment between two persons. As the Bible says, *"beauty is fleeting."* The sexual excitement and physical attraction of a person to an opposite gender might wane with time, especially when the flaws of an individual come to the surface.

2. Philia

Philia is another form of love that is commonly defined as the warm affections and caring emotions shared by friends. *Philia* is the root word for *philosophy* which literally means love of wisdom and *philanthropy* which means love of fellow man. If *Eros* mostly pertains to sexual feelings for another person, *Philia* on the other hand metaphorically speaks about the love that we feel for our friends and other important people in our lives. Our love for them is not caused by sexual attraction, but rather a deeper sense of care and kindness for all the things that they have done for us.

With regards to commitment, *Philia* can be considered as a stronger form of love because it doesn't come from things that fade like physical beauty. People who share *Philia* with each other care for the welfare of each other. This trait is something that you might not feel to a person that you don't really like.

3. Storge

This form of love is about the love between family members. For instance, if a parent told his child that he loves him, what he means is that he loves him in *Storge* form. Though, not exactly related to marital relationships, *Storge* will also provide insights about the emotions that we feel for our siblings, parents, children, and every member of the family that we care about.

4. Agape

According to the *Greco-Christian* terminologies about love, *Agape* is the highest form of love. It is usually used to describe a kind of love that is selfless, self-sacrificing, or unconditional. This kind of love doesn't look at the physical stature of a person, it is also not based on the care and affection that we received from other people and it is not about the love that we feel for the members of the family. *Agape* is an unconditional form of love that moves people into action an expression of love even without receiving anything in return. In the Bible, *Agape* is the word used to describe the love that God has for mankind.

In terms of a marital relationship, the *Agape* kind of love is that which is unconditional. It means that the love that each spouse has for each other has already transcended the *Eros* and *Philia*. *Agape* is the type of love that will further strengthen the commitment that the couple have for each other. If there will be problems and trials, if there are mistakes and sins that are done along the way, *Agape* will motivate the two persons to settle their differences, talk about the problem, and forgive each other of the mistakes that they committed.

All married couples must strive to have *Agape* in their relationships. It is not enough that you are just physically attracted to each other. It is not also enough that you care about your spouse as a friend would – a companionate love. What is needed for a lasting and strong marriage is the unconditional love for each other. However, I will not be quick to note that *Eros* is wrong. In fact, there will be no marriages if there are no physical attractions that happened between the couples early in their relationship. The point here is that spouses must not be contented on staying on that level of their relationship. Instead, they must work towards accepting each other's flaws and shortcomings while at the same time growing in more love by noting any positive traits that their spouse have.

How to Grow Deeply in Love?

I personally believe that each couple must strive to have and sustain an *Agape* kind of love. However, the question is this: *How can I grow from just being physically attracted to my partner to loving him unconditionally?* And indeed, this is not an easy question to answer. There are a lot of factors that you need to consider when talking about love. You won't just read a book and wake up the next morning with unconditional love for your husband. It is a process. And it is a process that serious couples must go through. Here are three simple suggestions that you can consider if you want to grow deeper in love in your relationship:

1. Love Decisively

I know a lot of people who love their partners out of their emotions. This phenomenon is especially notorious during the initial stages of love where the *crazy form of love* is at work and the *"love chemicals"* in the brain are being produced in torrential gush. However, when the emotion wanes, these couples are quick to assume that the love is also gone. Their love for each other is built on the feelings that they have. It is superficial, indeed. Thus, it is crucial that we love decisively, which means that our love must be based on not only our emotions but on our decisions.

In a recent survey conducted, it was determined that about 91% of women and 86% of men in America believe that romantic love is an essential component of marriage. But the truth that we need to understand is that romantic love doesn't necessarily equate to crazy love, it doesn't matter what you feel – whether your heart is pounding right off your chest, or your hands are getting sweatier by the minute, or you can just feel that time slows down whenever you are with her. Love must transcend our emotions on the surface, instead it must be rooted in the decisions that we made underneath. That is one secret to have the unconditional kind of love.

When your love is based on your decision, then you will continue loving your spouse no matter how you feel. Let's face it, things will not always happen the way we had planned and marriage is not an exception. Problems and troubles will come crashing to tear down your relationship, but if you have already made the decision to stick to it, then you can have a stronger anchor to weather the storms of life. Therefore, love decisively.

2. Love Intimately

If you are married for several years, when was the last time that you did something romantic for your spouse? When was the last time that you gave him an unsolicited massage? When was the last time that you gave her a bouquet of flowers? When was the last time that you spent time together as if there is no tomorrow? Study shows that couples tend to grow apart as their marriage gets older. It means that they talk less, spend time less, and even express their love less. Intimacy keeps decreasing instead of growing steadily.

Strong commitment is built on deep intimacy with each other. Think about this: *Would you allow yourself to stay with a person that is becoming more of a stranger to you every day?* Logically, the answer is *"No."* When intimacy is removed from the equation of marriage and both spouses grow apart from each other, then commitment tends to weaken too. And before they know it, one party might have already started to have affair with another person – someone who listens more, someone who shows genuine interest, someone who communicates with warmth and appreciates his intelligence or her beauty.

But how can you deepen your intimacy with a person who's been with you for two decades? Is there anything new to learn from her? Is there anything that you might not still know about her? These are the common questions most people ask when it comes to being intimate in marriage – especially those already in a long-term marital relationship.

I heard a story about a couple who have been married for 30 years. Both of them are just going through the motions. They don't hate each other, but at the same time, they don't love each other as they have been in love before. Then, upon going to a marriage counselor, they found out that the problem is that they are not communicating in the love language of one another. While the husband wants to feel loved by having his wife serve him, the wife wants to feel the love of his husband by spending time with her. The marriage counselor gave them some things to implement, and months after, they are like a young couple again.

Keeping the intimacy in marriage whether it's emotional or physical is not an easy thing to do. You need to spend time to talk about it and identify the source of the deteriorating intimacy between you. Perhaps, like the couple above, you are just speaking the wrong language of love of each other. Or maybe, there are some unsettled issues that were just brushed off in the past that strained the relationship. Or perhaps, you just don't feel it anymore, both of you don't want to be intimate because you know that it will be hard work.

Whatever the reason is, you can be intimate again; you just need to work at it. Try to understand the language of love of your spouse. Open up and bring to the table any unsettled issues that you have between you. And remember, love must be based on decision, not on emotions. Love your spouse even if you don't *'feel'* like doing it. In the end, the rewards of an intimate marriage will benefit you greatly and improve, not just your relationship, but the affection inside the family as well.

3. Love Unconditionally

Like every decision that we make in our lives, our decision to love unconditionally is always a choice that we need to consciously make. It is a reality that your spouse might not be loveable at specific moments in your relationship. There could be those times where all you see are the flaws and imperfections of your partner, that all you are talking about are those negative things. There will also be those moments that one of you must give more than what she is receiving. Perhaps her love for her spouse is not being reciprocated at the same level. There's no denying that it could happen. But the essence of having the unconditional love is this: *loving the person no matter what.*

The *Agape* kind of love is the love that is used to describe the love of God in the Bible. It is the kind of love that is used in one of the most popular verses in the Bible said, *"For God so loved the world that He gave His one and only Son, that whoever believes in Him shall not perish but have everlasting life." (John 3:16)* Based on the Scriptures' narrative, man has been sinful and rebellious ever since the world has been created. It started with Adam and Eve then flowed through from generations to generations. The Lord based on His sense of justice and holiness knows that there must be punishment for this people and they don't deserve any love at all. Yet, God still chose to love them and displayed His unconditional love by sending Jesus to die on the cross, receive the punishment that is due from us, and using His death to draw people back to Him.

That is the true essence of unconditional love. In terms of marital relationship, unconditional love speaks of mercy, grace, and forgiveness. It is also about accepting each other in spite of the things that they have done in the past that caused pain and suffering. It is also about paving the way to reconciliation even if you are the person who has been offended. The Apostle Paul said something in his Epistle to the Ephesians that captures the need for spouses to love each other unconditionally. He said, *"Husbands, love your wives, just as Christ loved the church and gave himself up for her... each one of you also must love his wife as he loves himself, and the wife must respect her husband." (Ephesians 5:25, 35)*

The 5 Love Languages

Love is a central foundation of great and successful marriage. Every couple who wants to build an enduring and satisfying marital relationship must not lose their perspective when it comes to the importance of love in their union. However, it is also an established fact that a lot of spouses today say that they don't feel the same intensity and level of love anymore from their partners – especially for those couples who have been married for a couple of years. Though there are a lot of factors that surround this issue, one particular factor that appears again and again is the failure of husbands and wives to communicate to their spouses using their love language.

Dr. Gary Chapman wrote a book that is entirely dedicated to this specific matter. It is entitled, *"The 5 Love Languages: The Secret to Love that Lasts."* The main thesis of this book is that every individual has their own love language. The same with their mother tongue or native language, their love language is the way that they understand love and it is also the way that they express love to other people. The idea is you must speak in his or love language for that person to feel loved and appreciate your affection. Failure to speak in his or her love language won't communicate your love no matter how much effort you put into it. Dr. Chapman identified five major love languages that could be perceived by different people. These five love languages are briefly discussed below:

1. Words of Affirmation

Some people feel most loved when their partner affirm them. Kind and encouraging words make them feel appreciated. Saying *"I love you," "You are beautiful," "I adore you," and "I care for you"* works like magic when it comes to making them feel loved. It is not enough that you show your love through your actions, for those people who have this love language, you must tell it and speak it out.

An unhappy wife who has this love language is perhaps not receiving enough affirmation from her spouse. The man might be doing anything in his power to provide for the family and bring her gifts and flowers, but because she is not hearing those words of affirmation, she might still feel unloved.

2. Acts of Service

This love language is all about doing something and exerting actual effort, such as doing laundry, mowing the lawn, or cleaning the house to prove to them that you love them. For those people who have this love language, they believe in the axiom that *"action speaks louder than words."* Their love thrives on seeing acts of service from their spouse. And they appreciate actual action and help from their partners than intimate hugs and kisses, or other expressions of love.

3. Receiving Gifts

For other people, the best way to communicate that you love them is by giving them gifts. They feel the appreciation and affection of their partners when they receive something valuable from them. It means that those individuals who have this love language will prefer to receive a bouquet of flowers than hearing sweet words from their partners.

4. Quality Time

Persons who have this love language measure the love of their partners by looking at how they spend time together. They feel intimate with their spouse when they can give their undivided attention to each other. For them, the greatest measure of love is giving time – not just time, but quality time to each other.

5. Physical Touch

Love is communicated to those people with this love language by giving them appropriate touch. A tight hug, a kiss on the cheeks, and holding hands while walking is their idea of the expression of love. For married couples, sexual intercourse can even be a measure of how much love you have for each other.

Learning the love language of your spouse is crucial if you want her to appreciate your affection and the intimacy that you want to communicate to her. Here's one of the most crucial part of the principle of the 5 Love Languages: You and your spouse might have different love language and the way that you will express your love to your partner will depend on the love languages that you have.

For instance, if your love language is *Words of Affirmation,* then you are most likely to speak out words of affection to your spouse regularly because that is your idea of the best expression of love. You feel most loved when other people are affirming you through their words, and you might assume that it's how all people communicate their love to other persons. On the other hand, if your spouse's love language is *Quality Time,* then she will express her love by spending time with you and giving you her undivided attention. In the same way, she might assume that it is how all people communicate their love and therefore will expect you to do the same – if you truly love her.

Based on this theoretical framework, failing to speak in her love language – in spite of the abundance of expression in other love languages – will leave you both frustrated and wanting love. Let's say for example that your love language is *Acts of Service,* so you express your love by doing household chores and giving your best to make sure that your family has enough financial resources to support the daily expenses. As a natural user of this love language, you might also expect your spouse to do the same. However, your partner's love language is *Quality Time,* she loves to spend time with you and just wants to concentrate and give you her undivided attention whenever you are together. In the same way, she expects you to do the same.

However, because of your different love language, you might always be out there doing chores, while she just sits there waiting for you to finish so you can spend time together uninterrupted. Can you see the possible conflict that might arise eventually? You might say, *"You don't love me anymore! You just sit there while I do all these things."* To which she might fire back, *"No. You're the one who doesn't love me anymore! All you do are these chores! Can't we just spend time together?"* They are just expressing their love in their own love language and expecting their spouse to reciprocate, but because they have different love languages, conflict pops up. Thus, it is crucial for couples to understand the love language of each other and communicate appropriately.

Cohabitation: Kryptonite of Commitment

Commitment to each other is indeed one of the most important pillars of marriage. And it is essential for the spouses and even the society itself to strengthen that pillar by upholding commitment in marriage. The vows that the husband and wife make at the altar saying that they won't part for better or for worse must not just be words in a ceremony, instead, those phrases must guide their marital relationship and help them to build the commitment that they have for each other.

However, in spite of the importance of commitment to each other in a marriage, it is also a known fact that more and more people are going through the painful process of divorce. Marriages are getting destroyed, families are being torn apart and the society is going more liberal in its approach to marital relationships and unions. Indeed, the sanctity of marriage is under attack. In order to counter this phenomenon, some people have settled for cohabitation which is primarily motivated by the partner's desire to stay together without the need to formally sign a marriage contract.

The number of couples who are choosing to cohabitate have increased by 900% over the last 50 years. In fact, in America, the census data from 2012 showed that there are 7.8 million couples who are not yet married but are now living together. This figure is significantly higher compared to 2.9 million cohabiting couples in 1996. Cohabitation has become a precursor even for 2/3 of couples who got married in 2012 where they admit to living together for more than two years before tying the knot eventually.

Most people who approved of cohabitation reasoned: if cars are being taken to test drives before making the decision to buy, isn't this approach applicable also for marriage? A person might say, *"If I'm to make a decision that will alter the course of the remaining years of my life, then I ought to make that decision right. And I can only do that if I will test the relationship before deciding to get married. In that way, I can learn more about my partner and see if we are really compatible. If all goes well, then we can get married."*

But does cohabitation really improve marriages? Does the act of cohabiting before marriage strengthen the commitment that a couple have for each other? Is cohabitation the answer that we are looking for in order to make marriage lasting? For most people, the answers are all the informative, but what does studies and research about the concept of cohabitation really say? Here are some essential truths that were determined from various studies about cohabitation and in comparison with marriage .

1. The Sense of Security is lower in Cohabiting Couples than in Married Couples

Marriage was designed to provide a lot of physical and health benefits that may not be evident in couples who are cohabiting. A recent study conducted by Jim Koan from the University of Virginia was able to identify that there is a big difference between the conceptualisation of relationship between married and cohabiting partners. The results of the study suggested that the sense of security is considerably lower for cohabiting couples than for married partners.

Koan said, *"Asserting cohabitation is basically asserting that one is not 'locked in' to a commitment whereas marriage sends a signal of dependability and predictability. The take home implication is that our brains are sensitive to signs that the people we depend on in our lives are predictable and reliable. And our brains will depend upon – will, in effect, outsource to – those we feel are most predictable and reliable for our emotion-regulation needs."* In short, cohabiting couples are less secured with each other compared to couples who are married and the major differing factor is their expressed commitment to each other.

2. Cohabiting Couples are less likely to Get Married

According to a study released in 2015 by the Centre of Family and Demographic Research of the Sociology Department at Bowling Green State University's, modern cohabiting couples have lesser chance to get married compared to cohabiting couples 30 years ago. The researchers compared the stability of cohabiting couples today with those who engaged in cohabitation in the early 1980s. They also use the data from 707 women who cohabited in the distant past and 772 women who cohabited in the late 2000s.

They were able to ascertain that cohabitation last longer in the modern era, but this is due to the lessening number of cohabiting couples who transition in marriage. In fact, the couples today who are now living together without tying the knot are about half as likely to marry compared to couples who did the same thing in the 1980s. In addition, they are also more than 20% likely to separate.

3. Families of Cohabiting Couples are Less Stable than Married Couples

In addition to the weaker sense of security and the lessening possibility to get married, cohabiting couples also faced the danger of having a more unstable family for the children. This is the finding of an analysis released by the Institute for Family Studies (IFS) and the Social Trends Institute (STI) where it compared the effect of cohabitation vs. marriage in terms of the stability of a child over his first 12 years. The analysis studied families in more than 60 countries in order to properly identify the consequence of cohabitation in the family.

The study says that American and European children whose parents are just cohabiting by the time of their birth up to 12 years are more likely to see their parents get separated. IFS senior fellow W. Bradford Wilcox said, *"In more than 60 countries, we see that the rise in cohabitation is linked to an increase in family instability for children. It suggests there's something about marriage as an institution that signals commitment."* The study also indicated that children in America and 17 European countries, who were born to cohabiting couples, are 96% more likely to see their parents split compared to those children who were born to married couples.

In fairness to the concept of cohabitation, some recent studies also showed that cohabitation doesn't result to an increased rate of divorce. It means that cohabiting couples will not necessarily be involved in divorce. Yet, it still couldn't give the sense of security, the emotional and physical benefits, and the stability of family that marriage can give. Cohabitation might help you to avoid the sacrificial level of commitment that marriage requires, however, it will also steal from you the tremendous benefits – physically, emotionally, and psychologically – that could be provided to you by marriage.

Building Commitment

Commitment is rapidly becoming a rare commodity in every aspect of the modern society. And sadly, even in the arena of marriage. A lot of people are downplaying it and avoiding it because just the word itself carries a lot of weight and sense of responsibility. However, we cannot deny the fact that commitment will always be an essential pillar of successful relationships and marriages. Proving your love and committing yourself to another person under the vows of marriage is proven to bring a lot of advantages and benefits – these are gifts that are reserved only for those individuals who will choose to take the uphill road of commitment.

It is also important to note that commitment is not a one-time decision that will be finished once the rings are in place. Like every decision that we make, commitment demands us to work at it every day of our lives – to build and cultivate it. Each morning that we wake up presents us with a choice whether to uphold our commitment or to violate it. A simple glance at someone else, a playful chat with another person, or the simple act of removing the ring just to appear single might not hurt at the beginning, but soon enough, your weakening commitment will manifest itself in the deteriorating condition of your marriage. On the other hand, every act, no matter how simple it may seem that upholds your commitment can strengthen it and provide exponential benefits for you and your spouse. My friend, the choice is yours.

Reflection Questions:

This portion of each chapter aims to help you and your spouse to properly evaluate the principles and concepts that you have learned. Try to answer all the questions truthfully. Discuss it with your spouse so you can gain a greater insight when it comes to your partner's ideas and personal thoughts. It will also be helpful if you could share your answers with another couple who might be delighted to go in the journey with you.

1. In your own words, define the word, *"Commitment."* Try to elaborate the concept of commitment based on your own understanding. Afterwards, listen to the definition of your spouse. Are there any major differences about your views on commitment? If there are differences, why do you think your views on commitment differ and what is the source of those differing views?

   _____

   _____

   _____

2. On a scale of 1 to 10, 1 being the lowest and 10 being the highest, try to rate the level of your commitment to one another. The goal of this exercise is to identify any areas of your marriage that needs to be improved in relation to the criterion of commitment. Identify specific instances in your relationship that became the basis of your rating. If you are not happy and satisfied with the score that you have given yourself when it comes to commitment, then identify the actions that you must take to improve the score and to display your commitment to each other.

   _____

   _____

   _____

3. In this chapter, we discussed the importance of love in relationship and its significant effect on the level of commitment that you have for each other. We also discussed that love between spouses must improve into a form of *Agape.* In your honest assessment, can the level of love between you now be considered as *Agape?* If yes, then determine specific instances that prove your *Agape* love to each other. If not, then what level are you at right now? What actions will you take to grow your love into *Agape?*

_____

_____

4. Based on our discussion of the 5 Love Languages, what do you think is your love language and what is the love language of your spouse? There is a free assessment that you can try out in this link: http://www.5lovelanguages.com/profile/ I would also recommend that you purchase the book of Dr. Gary Chapman to get a better insight about love languages. For now, one clue that might point strongly to your love language is the way you are expressing your love to other people and to your spouse. Try to list down 5 instances that display that this is indeed your love language.

_____

_____

_____

5. Cohabitation is becoming a popular method of testing the relationship before moving on to marriage. In your honest opinion, what do you think about cohabitation? Do you believe that it is okay for couples to try it out first or to have a *test drive* before committing to each other in marriage? What do you think is the main advantages and disadvantages of cohabitation?

_____

_____

SECOND CRITERION: HEALTHY COMMUNICATION

CHAPTER 4

"Everyone should be quick to listen,
slow to speak and slow to become angry."

– James 1:19 (NIV)

A lot of studies and research have been conducted to identify the reasons why a lot of couples divorce. Several explanations were forwarded. Mental health professionals, marriage counsellors and pastors share their own ideas and insights about the causes of divorce. A study was conducted in 2013 by the experts in Tango Media Corporation to identify the primary reason of couples splitting up. 100 mental health professionals were surveyed and asked certain questions in relation to divorce of married couples.

The results of the survey are quite revealing. First, they were able to conclude that the Number 1 way to improve your marriage and avoid the pain and inconvenience of divorce is by improving the communication between spouses. This conclusion is due to the fact that 65% of divorce noted by the surveyed professionals was caused by severe communication problems. Also, the complaints differ between husbands and wives with regards to communicating with each other. 70% of men sited nagging and complaining as a serious problem in communication that might lead to divorce. On the other hand, 83% of women said that their communication problem arose from their spouse not validating their feelings and opinions, followed by 56% of wives who said that their partners do not know how to listen but rather they talk about themselves too much.

WHAT CAN I DO TO MAKE MY MARRIAGE WORK?

The health of the relationship of married couples is undeniably anchored on the health of communication between them. There are a lot of factors that might cause divorce, but poor communication magnifies the problem by tenfold. Thus, it is crucial for couples to learn the fundamental principles of healthy communication. In fact, I would go as far to say that when couples learn how to communicate effectively to each other, the chances of divorce are drastically lowered.

In this Chapter, we will discuss about the basic ideas and concepts relating to healthy communication in marriage. We will start by looking at the different levels of communication that we usually engage in our everyday lives. After that, we will go over to the different types of communication that couples normally use within the boundary of their relationship. We will also look at the tremendous benefits that strong connection between spouses could bring to marriage. And lastly, we will discuss the different rules that each spouse must follow to ensure that their communication and consequently, their marriage, is always in its best shape.

Different Levels of Communication

We started to communicate from the time that we were born and were made aware of our ability to connect with people around us through the medium of communication. In fact, according to studies, an average woman will speak about 20,000 words a day while an average man will speak of 7,000 words a day. We meet a lot of people in a day and we actively engage in communication with some of them. However, we instinctively know that our level of communication with individuals will largely depend on our relationship and previous interaction with those people.

For instance, we usually don't talk to strangers and in those rare instances that someone comes up to us and talks about something; we normally don't share to them our experiences and the things that we feel. On the other hand, when it comes to people who are truly close to us, we can be really comfortable in opening up to them the deepest emotions that we have in our hearts. In relation to this concept, we need to understand the levels of communication that we have with different people in our lives. This discussion will be helpful in knowing whether we are having some limitations when it comes to talking with our spouse and thus set a platform to improve our communication within the marital relationship.

Level 1: Stranger Level

The first level of communication is called the stranger level. It consists of small talks about the weather, about current events, news and other things that might be popularly known in our lives. The communication within this level is mostly superficial and limited only to facts. We usually communicate at this level when talking with strangers or new acquaintances. Also, at the stranger level, we are trying to find some common ground with the people we talk to so we can move on to higher levels of communication.

Level 2: Acquaintance Level

The second level of communication can be called the acquaintance level. This level involves talking about basic facts about ourselves and what we do for a living, brief opinion, popular perspective about some things, strategies and tips, especially when the person we are talking with is on the same field as ours. Though this level is slightly deeper than the stranger level, the difference between the two is not that great. Since the topics inside the acquaintance level mostly vent on things that can be validated by studies and general knowledge, there is no need to be involved in deepening opinions and deeper considerations.

Level 3: Friendly Level

The friendly level of communication can be considered the third level. This is the level where two people can talk about their deep-seated beliefs and perspectives. They can also share about their wants, needs, fears, joys and the way that they feel at that particular moment. This level is reserved for close friends and family. We can also use this level of communication when talking with mentors, church mates, and people who have grown closer to us over time. Though there are still things that we are holding back from the individuals at this level, the difference between the third level and the first two levels is significantly greater.

Level 4: Spouse Level

The fourth level of communication is what we can call the spouse level. At this level, the intimacy, trust and transparency between two people is the foundation of the communication. When talking with your spouse, you must make sure that there is no hindrance in expressing each other's emotions and thoughts in every aspect of your life. In fact, I believe that other than God, your spouse should be the only person that you share all the intimate details of your life with. Your partner should be the only individual who knows all your vulnerabilities, persistent fears, and source of joy.

For you to have a better understanding of the concepts involved, here's a brief example of how the four levels of communication differ from one another. Let us use the illustration of talking about the weather.

Level 1: According to weather forecasts, it will rain later this afternoon.

Level 2: According to weather forecasts, it will rain later this afternoon. I guess we should bring our umbrella, what do you think?

Level 3: According to weather forecasts, it will rain later this afternoon. Oh, I can't explain, but I'm so excited! It hasn't rained for quite some time.

Level 4: According to weather forecasts, it will rain later this afternoon. I'm so excited. Do you still remember the story that I told you how I really love the rain when I was a child?

The Source of Conflict

Communicating with different people in our lives is essential to our survival and sanity. Even the most introverted person has a need to communicate with someone over the course of his reclusive life. Though communication is crucial, conflicts and frustrations might arise if we interchange the levels with those people we connect with. Let me give you some examples.

Imagine that you are meeting someone for the first time, and since you are not conscious of the levels of communication, you proceed to talk with that individual about all the intimate details in your life. Let's say that you start immediately on Level 3. What do you think the other person will think as you share your fears, your dreams and your emotional experiences within your family with that person in the first few minutes of your meeting? I believe that person will feel most uncomfortable. He just met you and you don't even have the foundation of friendship to talk about such things.

Let's try another one. What do you think will happen if you share Level 4 communication with another person other than your spouse? You are sharing the intimate details of your life, your family, your frustrations, and everything that is going on around you. A friend of mine, who was already engaged, did this level of communication with another lady. The lady has problems and issues so she shared those things with my friend, and my friend did the same. And before they knew it, they found themselves falling for each other. There is a principle in human psychology which holds that we will be drawn and feel closer to those people who are transparent to us. My friend probably didn't know about this and his ignorance of that principle caused him his three years relationship.

The 4 Levels of Communication is meant to guide us in our interaction with people in our lives. We must speak and communicate with people based on our relationship with them. This idea will help us to put into proper perspective our interactions with other people while at the same time protect the most important relationship that we have, which is our relationship with our partner.

Different Types of Communication

Since having a healthy communication is one of the most powerful deterrents of divorce, it is highly important to gain some knowledge and skills when it comes to connecting with one another. In addition to the Level 4 communication in marital relationships, marriage couples must also learn about the types of communication that can happen inside the marriage. This concept will give them an idea of how they can communicate naturally inside the relationship without feeling forced, pressured or exhausted by the Level 4 Communication.

Small Talk

Small talk is great starter for conversations. You don't want to meet your spouse after a long day's work and immediately gush out all your emotional experiences during the day. It will be both shocking and frustrating to be bombarded with a lot of loaded information when all you want to do is to sit and spend a few minutes to rest together with your spouse. Small talk about the weather, about the travel and whether your spouse wants a cold-drink of water are great ideas to start the conversation.

Emotional Conversation

This communication is all about talking what you and your spouse feel at the moment with regards to certain aspects of your relationship or your individual life. I would suggest that you regularly talk about the things bothering you and the things that make your hearts leap with joy. Share your frustrations, your anger and your struggles. Celebrate your wins, victories, and your future aspirations. Whatever it is, just make it a point to talk about those things that weigh heavily on your heart. Emotional conversation is at the heart of Level 4 Communication because you should only talk on these things with your spouse.

There was a couple who have been married for several years now. Their communication can be considered healthy because they always talk about a lot of things. In the course of time, the husband became a sought-after speaker and author that is popular across America. A lot of exciting things happened in his life and whenever he stumbled upon a great idea or a nugget of wisdom, he couldn't wait to share it with other people. However, upon coming home, the excitement to share that idea will diminish because he already shared it with the people around him. Therefore, they didn't have something exciting to talk about.

The husband became aware of what's happening and did something to solve the dilemma. When he learned of something new, he wouldn't share it to other people immediately. Instead, he would wait until he's home with his wife and she will be the first to learn the new thing before he even shared it with other people. This way, the husband shared the excitement to her wife and their relationship benefited from it.

Emotional conversations are important aspects of marital communication. A lot of couples, especially those who have been together for several years, always ask this question: *"Are there things still to learn from my spouse? We have been talking for years now and I think I know her enough. Is there something new that we can talk about?"* And one suggestion is to talk about your emotions because emotion is never constant. The way you feel today might not be the same way that you will feel tomorrow. You might feel accomplished today, but there is no guarantee that you will still feel that way next week. When couples talk about their emotions, they are always talking about something new.

Conference Conversation

As we have discussed in the previous chapters, disagreements between spouses are inevitable. It will always be a part of marital relationships and therefore must be weathered effectively. In fact, if lack of healthy communication is the number one cause of divorce according to the survey conducted by Tango Media Corporation, the inability of married couples to resolve conflict ranks as second. Most of the time, the way the couple argue cause more damage to the relationship than the original reason for the fight.

During the height of emotions, individuals have the tendency to call names, disregard the emotions of the other person, and say hurtful words when venting anger. This, I believe, is not the right way to resolve conflicts and disagreements. And this will bring us to another type of communication between spouses that can be considerably useful. It's the *Conference Conversation*. It draws the idea between conference meetings between two parties who are trying to iron out a deal. In a conference, both parties have the allotted time to discuss each agenda. And during the discussion of one of the parties, the other party will try his best to understand the subject matter being discussed while taking note of some areas of confusion to be asked at the end of the discussion.

The *Conference Conversation* between spouses shares the same idea. When there is disagreement, conflict and any issue that needs to be resolved, each individual will have his or her own take on the matter; this type of communication must be put in use. Determine the first person who will speak. Let's assume for a while that it's the wife to talk, the husband must patiently listen to the explanations and reasons of her spouse while taking notes of some points of questions to ask later. After the wife, it is now the husband's turn to explain and discuss his own view on the matter. After this first turn, round two will begin but this will focus on question and answers until both parties came to an agreement.

This type of communication to settle disagreements is a good idea to argue and still love each other at the same time. However, there are some rules that must be followed when using *Conference Conversation*. First, listen to understand not to respond. Second, avoid attacking the person; instead mention what you feel because of the actions of that person. Third, don't do this in the height of your emotion, there should be a few minutes of cooling off period just to let down some steam from the arguments.

Destructive Communication

This type of communication is the exact opposite of the *Conference Conversation*. When couples engage in *Destructive Communication*, they are mostly focusing on the pain and hurt that was caused by the other party. They do not really care about what the other person feels and the main goal of both partners is to hurt and take revenge from what he or she suffered. This type of communication will not necessarily destroy the relationship in one single blow. However, as the pain and heartache accumulate, the

Destructive Communication will also snowball until it becomes a massive weapon that will surely destroy the relationship.

Couples must be wise and be aware when a *Destructive Communication* is on its way. Here are some signs that you can look out for. First, no one wants to give way and listen. Since both parties are being driven by emotion and believe that they are in the right, no one wants to let up and listen. They yell at the top of their voice in order to gain ground and take control of the conversation. Second, there are a lot of name callings and abusive language. In this kind of communication, anger reigns supreme and therefore must be given free vent. The destructive kind of anger doesn't distinguish between hurtful words and offensive arguments. Third, regrets will creep up after the argument but it will be too hard to forgive considering the word that was said.

You might already have heard of the proverb that says, *"Stick and stones may break my bones, but words will never hurt me."* This statement is false because we all know how words can penetrate deep within our beings and crush us from the inside. In fact, after all the bruises and wounds are gone, the obnoxious and foul statements that we received from the other person will stay and torment us. The situation will be the same for those people who receive hurtful words from us. We might receive their forgiveness and be okay on the surface, but deep inside the recesses of the human soul lies those cruel statements.

You must also consider the fact that we cannot take back the words that we say. When you say something, you are bound by the words that you have just uttered. Therefore, it is of utmost importance to think twice before saying anything to your spouse. Let the emotions cool off before talking to each other. Take a brief walk, do some exercise; shout at the top of your voice outside. Whatever it is, do anything in your power to lower down your emotions before engaging in an argument with your spouse.

''If all couples can master the art of communication in their marriages, most issues will not see the light of day'' Chindah Chindah

Why Cultivate Healthy Communication?

We have established in the proceeding discussions that having a healthy connection between spouses through the lines of open communication could greatly enhance the marital relationship while helping to reduce the possibility of having a divorce. In addition to these tremendous benefits that are provided by great communication between partners, there are several positive reasons why you should strive to cultivate a strong and loving communication lines between you and your spouse. Here are some of these reasons:

Deeper knowledge about each other

People are all created unique by God. We all have our individual quirks and idiosyncrasies that are entirely unique to us. We also have a wealth of experience, wisdom from the things that happened to us, and even an entire myriad of emotions that we display all throughout our lives. A person's being is like a mystery waiting to unfold. It is also similar to a deep ocean that invites another person to explore. However, the mysteries of this deep well of the soul can only be discovered when another person decides to uncover it and this is done by having communication.

When a couple are new in their relationship, both of them do not know much from each other. Their communication as acquaintances will revolve around those things that might interest them but they tend to consciously avoid those topics that might reveal the true person inside them. As the relationship progresses to friendship, they might now be able to share their opinions, experiences and emotions. The revelation at this particular stage might be a determining factor whether both of them will decide to continue their relationship. If they decide to give it a go, then they will reveal more and more of themselves - the deep anguish of the past, those things that makes their hearts beat fast, even the things that they dream about.

All these things that a couple reveal about each other are mainly done through the medium of communication - some text the whole day, others talk on the phone till midnight. And there are individuals who are setting aside a particular day or time of the week just to talk with that one person. Communication is essential for couples to know their partners better. However, as we all know, more often than not, the frequency and depth of communication between spouses gets lower and shallower as time goes by. Yet, if you desire to have a deeper knowledge about one another, then you need to spark the interest to know more on the experiences, emotions and dreams of your partner once again. And healthy communication is the key in doing just that.

Stronger Bond and Relationship

Can you imagine going home one day with a sheer feeling of excitement to meet your spouse? There were a lot of things that had happened to you throughout the day and you can't wait to share everything with her. So you left the office on time and drove fast to arrive home early. Upon coming home, you immediately parked the car on the front yard, went straight to the door and opened it. And there she was, waiting on the table, the food was ready, and she flashed that crooked smile that you both know too well. You walked towards her, then you said, *"Honey... You won't believe what happened in the office today!"* She smiled and blushingly said, *"Aren't you forgetting something?"* *"Oh! Of course!"*, you exclaimed, as you kissed her on the lips. And then you immediately gushed out, *"Honey! You won't believe what happened in the office today!"* To which she replied, *"Alright, honey, tell me about it."* And you talked for five hours that night just learning what happened to each of you.

That's a great picture of communication between spouses, wouldn't you agree? And I hope you would also approve that this kind of communication can help create a stronger bond and relationship for couples in marriage. However, as you all know, for a lot of married partners today, this stuff is just like an advertisement. In short, it's just a figment of imagination. Instead of meaningful conversations, spouses are talking in grunts, *"Uh-huh,"* and other words that communicate nothing but a basic lack of interest. But it is not too late to change this situation. If both partners will just take the time to be interested and intentional in their conversation, then they can also build a stronger bond and relationship for their marriage.

Think about this. There are two couples who have been married for five years now. They still don't have kids and both are working on separate companies in the city capitol. The couples are pretty much alike in every aspect of their relationship except in terms of communication. The first couple decided to consistently talk to each other. Whatever happens during the day, they will talk about it even if all they can share is the mundane tasks that they did at work. They want to build a strong culture of transparency and authenticity in their relationship. In fact, they agreed to share even the negative emotions that they have with each other. If there is one word to describe their relationship in terms of communication, it's *intentional.*

On the other hand, the second couple don't really have a plan when it comes to the communication aspects of their relationship. Granted, they talk when there are major happenings like promotion, accident on the road, or irritating events while at work. However, unlike the first couple, their conversations are only limited to those subjects. When a day is just an *"ordinary"* day, they just simply shrug it off and say, *"Nothing extraordinary happened today. Perhaps, we can just rest for this day."* Now, considering the status of their communication, which couple do you think will be better prepared when a trial hits the relationship? The first couple who have built a solid and strong communication lines or the second couple who can be considered as *"occasional communicators?"*

Growing Intimacy and Love

Do you want to deepen your love for your spouse? Do you want to know how you can love him better? Do you want to discover one of the secrets of growing intimacy? Well, my friend, it's simple. Talk frequently. And when I say talk, I'm not referring to those *"Grunt Conversations"* that a lot of couples are used to. I'm talking about the kind of talk that helps each person to feel appreciated, valued and loved. I'm talking about the kind of conversation between two people that enables them to show each other who they really are, what they really feel, and why they do feel a certain kind of way. Those kinds of communications are guaranteed to grow intimacy and love between couples.

If you fell in love with your spouse because of the things that you know about her, and the experiences you shared, then why don't you do more of it? If talking with one another when you were just starting the relationship helped you to cultivate intimacy, then you should also exploit its benefits today. Remember this, when you stop talking, intimacy stops growing, love will grow cold, and the relationship might be in jeopardy. How can I say that? Because as we have noted in the first part of this chapter, poor communication is one of the leading causes of divorce. So talk frequently, converse deeply and communicate warmly.

Communication Rules between Spouses

Several research and studies have been conducted with regards to the central role that healthy communication plays in the marital satisfaction between couples and indeed, it plays a central role. If you believe that healthy communication is an important key to have a successful marriage, then you should get better at it every single day of your married life. However, you must understand that getting better at communication skills will not automatically improve your chances of not getting divorced. That notion is just the surface of the arena of communication.

When it comes to conversation between spouses, there are fundamental principles that must be followed. These principles can be considered timeless and using it to improve your communication lines with your spouse will guarantee to improvement, not just the communication per se, but the entire relationship as well. Here are some suggested principles that you can use in order to improve on the communication aspect of marital partnership.

Be Intentional and Prepared

Good communication doesn't happen by chance. You won't just wake up one day and realize that your communication with your spouse is getting better by the minute. Healthy conversations are usually a result of intentionality and preparation. So, how can you become intentional? What are the things that you can try to help you in building rapport and connection with one another?

There are couples who are scheduling monthly dates, just the two of them, without the kids. It is just like the good old days when they were still two young lovers at the courtship stage. Other couples are preparing key questions that they can ask to each other while having their *"we-time"* together. And still other couples, who want to keep it simple, will just sit on a couch and just talk about the day. As you can see, all of these techniques require a huge amount of intentionality – from setting the date and time, organizing the schedule, preparing questions, and spending energy.

I don't know what will work for you and your partner, but the principle still holds true. In the aspect of communication, and in fact, in every other aspect of marriage, intentionality is always the key.

Be Slow to Speak but Quick to Listen

The Apostle James spoke of a wise advice when it comes to our communication affairs, and this advice is extra important when it comes to marital relationship. He said in James 1:19, *"My dear brothers and sisters, take note of this: Everyone should be quick to listen, slow to speak and slow to become angry."* They said that we have two ears and one mouth because we are meant to listen more than we talk.

However, most people got it the other way around. They love to talk more than to listen to what the other person has to say. John Maxwell loves to tell about this practical joke about his friend who loves to talk so much about himself. One day, Maxwell and his friend met. After exchanging pleasantries, his friend immediately talked about his favourite topic – himself. Maxwell patiently listened as his friend went on and on in his ramblings. And after several minutes, his friend exhaustedly said, *"Wait, John. I'm talking too much about myself, I'm sorry. I want to listen to you. Talk about me."*

A lot of individuals are too busy speaking that they forget to listen. And during those rare times that they choose to listen, they listen for the sake of responding to what the other person is saying and not in understanding it. So the next time that you communicate with your spouse, why not try to listen more? Here are some tips where you can begin. Alan Loy McGinnis in his book, *"The Friendship Factor,"* mentioned the characteristics of a good listener as listed below:

- Good listeners listen with their eyes.
- Good listeners dispense advice sparingly.
- Good listeners never break a confidence.
- Good listeners complete the loop. *(Respond accordingly to what the other person said. Don't answer with silence.)*
- Good listeners show gratitude when someone confides.

Be Entirely Focused

Imagine this scenario. The wife just had a very embarrassing moment in the grocery store. While picking up cans of tuna, several cans dropped from the top cabin and another shopper was hit. The shopper was furious, yelled at her and insulted her. The wife was so embarrass and though she apologizes, the shopper refused to stop and heaped offending remarks about her. The wife wanted to cry but she composed herself and went home.

She found her husband watching the TV and she immediately snuggled close to him. She said, *"Baby, you know what? Something embarrassing happened to me in the supermarket."* Her husband, still focused on what he was watching, just replied with an uninterested, *"Uh-huh."* Still, the wife continued, *"I was picking up this can of tuna and then several cans from the top cabin fell and hit another shopper."* *"Honey,"* the husband replied, *"can this wait? It's the last 10 seconds of the game. Hold on a bit."*

What do you think will the wife feel? There are a myriad of negative emotions that she might feel. And all of this is because the husband chose to focus on the television instead ofhis wife. She felt horrible. She thought that if there is one person who will understand and comfort her, it's her husband. Yet, all she got was an *"Uh-huh"* and a refusal to talk.

When engaging in communication with your spouse, it is utmost important to maintain focus. Turn off the TV. Put aside your phone. Give your spouse the undivided attention that she deserves. Listen attentively and respond accordingly. Validate her feelings, learn more about her. It will not only improve your communication and relationship, but it will also communicate how much you value your spouse.

Be Prepared to Talk about Everything

Perhaps, one of the most controversial topics when it comes to communication between spouses is keeping secrets to one another. Is it alright to keep some information to your partner? Is it acceptable to withhold your emotions and keep crucial details about the relationship or about what's happening to you to yourself?

A study was conducted by a group of psychologists and other mental health professionals from University of Tennessee and East Carolina University to understand the concept of secret-keeping in marital relationships. The research team was led by Beth Easterling. In an online surveys conducted for a group of females, mostly married and in a serious relationship, the researchers found out that about 60% of participants kept at least one secret to their partner at some point while about 25% said that they are currently keeping a secret.

People have reasons why they keep secrets and there are a wide variety of secrets that are being kept by spouses, but is it healthy for married partners to keep secret from one another? As we all know, one of the basic foundations of a strong and healthy marriage is trust and acceptance. And if partners will deliberately hold information to their partners, this might cause frustration and loss of trust. After all, how can you trust a person who doesn't trust you enough about his past and other embarrassing matters about his life?

As for my opinion, it is a good practice to regularly keep each other in check whether they are being truthful and honest to each other. One method that I believe will work effectively to facilitate this concept is to schedule a monthly date and prepare questions to ask about each other. In the list of questions, include the following: *What are the secrets that you are not telling me? Why are you withholding that particular information from me? Do you trust me enough that I can handle it?*

It might feel awkward at first because most people are still struggling with the art of self-disclosure even to the people they hold most dear. However, if you train yourself to do this exercise regularly, then I can guarantee that you will be able to avoid any major problems to develop. Yet, an important note, make sure that you are also prepared enough to handle what you might know by asking these questions.

Be Affectionate and Always Communicate Warmth

If there is one thing that is commonly being kept as a secret by spouses in marriage, it is their affection and appreciation from one another. This is not usually a problem by couples who are still early in their relationship. However, it is the contrary when talking about couples who are already in the relationship for a long time, especially if they have been spending a lot of their times managing the household affairs.

Another problem is that most people tend to act like mirrors. They will only reciprocate the kind words that they receive from their partners. Yet, the issue here is that, when they wait for each other, they might end up not receiving anything from one another. It is tragic, but it is true for a lot of couples today.

However, you can still do otherwise. Start now by complimenting your spouse. You don't have to be overly dramatic and utter cheesy pick-up lines, right then and there. You can just simply notice how nice her hair is, or maybe appreciate the smell of her perfume, or say a short thank you for everything that she is doing for the family. In the same way, wives can communicate their affections by acknowledging the hard work of their husbands. Be creative. Be expressive. Here's a tip: *Make it a goal to speak one kind word a day to your spouse.*

Be Mindful of Nonverbal Communication

Most people say that the majority of communication with other people is by using non-verbal cues and body language. According to Albert Mehrabian, 55% of communication is body language, 38% is the tone of voice, and 7% is the actual words spoken. Though, these numbers are contested, it is still highly believed in psychology circles that the way we act and the way we say things influenced greatly the things that we are communicating to other people.

For instance, have you ever talked to a person who is saying a lot of good things about you, but his facial expression, the way his body moves, and even the resolve in what he is saying says otherwise? Or have you ever talked to a person who says she is listening, but she doesn't look at you because she is too busy writing a text message in her chat application? And perhaps you are listening to your spouse, who says she is not mad at you, yet she can't look at you directly, and her body language is so stiff.

Indeed, the things that you say to your spouse won't really matter if your body language, facial expression and the tone of your voice don't match with what you are saying. Good communication is not just about the actual choice of words that you use. If you want to cultivate a healthy communication lines between you and your partner, then you also need to be mindful of your nonverbal cues.

Healthy Communication = Healthy Relationship

In a study conducted by Brant Burleson and Wayne Denton entitled, *"The Relationship between Communication Skill and Marital Satisfaction: Some Moderating Effects"* published in the *Journal of Marriage and Family,* they found out an interesting insight. They realized that happily married couples have the same level of communication skills with unmarried couples. Burleson and Denton defined communication skills as *"the proficiency in sending and receiving clear messages and the ability to accurately interpret the intent of each other's message. "* In short, it is about the capacity of the individuals to talk and understand one another.

However, it's surprising to learn that even if you can talk and understand one another, you can still be dissatisfied with your marriage. How is that possible? Burleson and Denton said that the difference that happily married couples has is their intentions and how they used their communication skills to connect with one another. Happily married couples talk with the positive intention of reaching out to their spouse while distressed married couples talk with a negative will about one another. Thus, it is not a matter of skill but of will.

The tips and techniques found in this chapter won't matter much if you will learn it just for the sake of learning it. Your communication skill can be considered neutral yet its effect will vary depending on your motives and intentions regarding your spouse. Let all your conversation – whether its normal chat or a conference on disagreement – be seasoned with love and affection. Remember, when you are able to cultivate healthy communication, you are also in the best position to cultivate a healthy relationship.

Reflection Questions:

This portion of each chapter aims to help you and your spouse to properly evaluate the principles and concepts that you have learned. Try to answer all the questions truthfully. Discuss it with your spouse so you can gain a greater insight when it comes to your partner's ideas and personal thoughts. It will also be helpful if you could share your answers with another couple who might be delighted to go in the journey with you.

1. How do you view communication? Do you believe in the principle which says that healthy communication will help to build a healthy relationship? On a scale of 1 to 10, how will you rate your communication with your spouse? 1 is the lowest and 10 is the highest? What is the reason for that rating? Go back to your conversation with your spouse for the last week; evaluate the things that you talk about and the length of time that you talk. On the four level of communication, on what level are you communicating for the last week?

_____

_____

_____

2. In this chapter, we discussed the four types of communication namely, the *Small Talk, Emotional Conversation, Conference Conversation* and *Destructive Communication.* Try again to review the conversations that you had for the last week and identify what type of communication you engaged in. Upon identifying the type of communication, evaluate the topic that you talked about as well as the reason why you chose to talk on that specific subject matter.

_____

_____

_____

3. There are great benefits that you can gain once you exert the effort needed to cultivate a strong and healthy communication between you and your spouse. Try to compare the frequency and depth of the communication that you have when you were just starting in the relationship and now that a number of years have already passed. Did it became lower and shallower, or the frequency grew and it also became deeper? What do you think is the benefit (*or the detriment*) of the change in the health of your communication?

_____

_____

_____

4. There are different principles in cultivating a healthy communication between individuals, especially between spouses. We have identified six of these principles which I repeated below:

- *Be intentional and prepared*
- *Be slow to speak but quick to listen*
- *Be entirely focused.*
- *Be prepared to talk about everything.*
- *Be affectionate and always communicate warmth.*
- *Be mindful of nonverbal communication*

What specific principle are you already applying to your communication with your spouse? What benefits have you reaped from applying that principle? What particular principle are you struggling to apply? What is the reason you're struggling in applying it? What is your plan to make it a part of your regular communication with your spouse?

_____

_____

_____

5. As mentioned on the research by Burleson and Denton, they conclude that healthy communication is more of a function of *"will"* than a function of *"skill."* Why do you think the intention and motives of each individual spouse matters when it comes to their communication? What steps will you take to ensure that you have the right intention at hand when trying to settle a matter or discuss a particular topic with your spouse?

_____

_____

_____

THIRD CRITERION:
THE ART OF CONSIDERATION

CHAPTER 5

*"Tolerance and celebration of individual
differences is the fire that fuels lasting love."*

– Tom Hannah

We are imperfect humans; that is a fundamental truth that we all agree to believe. At his core, an individual is full of weaknesses, flaws and blemishes. These imperfections tend to stain everything that we are trying to do or accomplish. In fact, every aspect of our lives is tainted with imperfections – and the wonderful gift of marriage is not an exception.

However, in spite of the fundamentality of the notion of an individual's imperfection, a lot of people are still holding to the principle that their spouse and accordingly, their marriage, must be perfect. A study was conducted by Mary Laner, a sociologist in Arizona State University to determine the expectation about marriage of unmarried college students. After getting their response, she compared the results with what couples who have been married for about 10 years have to say about the subject matter. And the result of the study just confirmed the disillusionment of unmarried people of what marriage truly is. They are expecting too much – a fairy tale, if you may. And *"Such irrationality,"* according to Laner, *"can lead us to conclude that when the thrill is gone, or when the marriage or partner doesn't live up to our inflated ideals, divorce or abandonment of that marriage in some form is the solution."*

Sadly, we allow ourselves to succumb to the idea that the perfect person – our soulmate – is just waiting out there to be found. And when destiny does its job right, we will find each other and spend the rest of our lives – happily ever after. Right? Wrong. Even the most beautiful love stories that we know, even those that are considered lasting, are full of imperfections. And if you are still dreaming of having a perfect marriage, then you are bound to be frustrated all your life because that dream will only be just a dream. Having a perfect marital relationship is like trying to lick your own elbows; it is – humanly speaking – impossible.

Considering these things, the need for couples to have a more realistic view of marriage is absolutely essential for marriage to work. If you are to confront the imperfections of the marital relationship and the flaws of your spouse, then you need to learn the *"Art of Tolerance."* That is what this chapter is all about. First we will talk about the reality of unfulfilled expectations and how most people respond when they come face to face with it. Next, we will elaborate on the fundamental principles and truth about marital relationships in relation to imperfections that will help you in dealing with the flaws of marriage. And lastly, I will share with you five top tips that you can implement in order to deal with imperfections in your relationship and your spouse.

The Reality of Marital Expectations

Let me ask you this question. Try to answer it as truthfully as you can because this question will reveal your core belief when it comes to your relationship with your spouse or how you view the idea of marriage as a whole. Here's the question: *What's your take on the idea of "Happy Ever After?"* If you have been reading books about princes and princesses' fairy tales, or have been watching movie with romantic themes, or you are just plainly a hopeless romantic, then I believe you have plenty of things that you can say regarding that topic.

For most people, that is what they are striving for. I know some ladies who are romantic dreamers. Ever since they were young, all they think about is how one day they will wear a beautiful, white, flowing wedding dress as they walk along the aisle to marry that ruggedly handsome man – the man of their dreams. After that, their husband will gladly lift them up in their arms as he carries her off to that gorgeous white lim and they ride towards the sunset – towards where everything is nice. And then the narrator will say, *"And they live happily ever after."*

I'm not passing judgment, if ever you are the kind of person who dream exactly just like that. Indeed, everyone wants their piece of romantic happiness and marital bliss. In fact, some are willing to let go of everything that they own just to have that. But in spite of what you want, there is a reality that you need to face when it comes to marital expectations because it plays a considerable part in marital satisfaction of both you and your spouse.

Expectations and Marital Satisfaction

In a study done by Cicile Rios entitled, *"The Relationship Between Premarital Advice, Expectations, and Marital Satisfaction"*, Rios tried to determine the dynamics that happen between the expectations before marriage of wedded couples and how they shape and affect the marital satisfaction that they have in their relationship. Rios also noticed the high degree of correlation between the two, thus justifying the need to create a more realistic expectation when entering marriage in order to be sufficiently satisfied with the relationship.

In other words, if your expectations are grounded on the wrong foundation, then your satisfaction with your marriage and your spouse will be negatively affected as well. On the contrary, if your expectations about marriage is optimistic and still realistic enough, then you are a candidate to experience satisfaction in your marital relationship. This theory is confirmed by another research done by Kristina Johnson where the dynamics between expectations and satisfaction in marriage was once again analysed. Johnson concluded that satisfaction in marital relationship is possible if the expectations are met. It doesn't matter if the expectations are set too high, or too low, the important factor is that all those expectations are being met. She said, *"whether one's expectations are fulfilled impacts marital satisfactions more than the height of their expectations."*

The Reality of Imperfections

Considering the results of the said studies, it is crucial to understand how expectations are being formed and the implication of setting the bar too high in order to be satisfied in marriage. For instance, going back to the allusion earlier to most people's fairy tale expectations of *"Happy Ever After,"* then we can conclude that a lot of individuals will accept nothing less than a near perfect relationship in marriage. And if any mistakes, heart aches, and problems can be found, then it might result to frustration and the wrong perception that perhaps, *"this relationship is not meant to be."*

If expectations play a crucial role in marriage satisfaction, then you also need to consider the reality of imperfections. As mentioned at the beginning of this chapter, we are imperfect humans and everything we do and anything that we participate in will be tainted by our flaws. Marriage will not always be *happy.* Marriage is not supposed to be perfect. And your spouse is not supposed to be that ideal prince or princess that never gets mad, never gets annoyed, and never stops showing how much has he or she cared for you. It doesn't happen in real life because we are living in an imperfect world.

Imperfections, mistakes and flaws are all realities of life, and the sooner you accept that nobody and no relationship can be perfect, then the earlier you can deal with that nudge in your mind about how dissatisfied you are with how your relationship is going. What I'm saying is that you should learn to set the expectations right. It doesn't mean, however, that we should just lower down our expectations just to be satisfied. Who can be satisfied living miserably in a run-down house where everything is plain eye-sore and all you do is argue the whole day about who should wash the dishes. I will discuss more of this topic later in this chapter.

The Usual Response to Imperfections

How do you usually respond when something does not go according to your plan? What goes on in your mind when everything that is happening is contrary to what you had originally envisioned it? How do you respond to your spouse when he does something annoying, when you are expecting him to be a fine gentleman with good manners and sound judgement? There could be myriads of responses to imperfections and here are the most common ones. Try to look out and reflect if that is how you respond too.

Offended

Sometimes, your mate will do something that is out of character of what you have envisioned him to be. Perhaps, he will say something that you've never heard from him before. Or maybe, he will act in a way that is totally strange and might remind you of someone who really annoys you in the past.

During these moments of imperfections, the usual response of most people is to feel offended. They put in a lot of thoughts to what was said and done and most of these thoughts are negative in nature. *"I didn't expect him to be that rude." "I thought she is thoughtful, how can she forget my birthday?" "I am willing to accept everything about him, but the things that he did earlier, that snuffed out the light in me."*

Nothing good ever comes out from a person that meditates an offense. Either he will take revenge, flee entirely from the situation or relationship, or just harbor resentment towards the person who committed the offense.

Regret

"I should have never have married you. You are not what I expected you to be." Regret is another negative response of individuals when it comes to the imperfection of their partners or even with another people. A lot of things will be

revealed in the initial stage of marriage, including the good and the bad.

Now, most people have the tendency to highlight the bad and completely forget the good. Couple this tendency with the passing of the intoxicating love, and now you are face with a decreasing feelings of intimacy and increasing emotions of annoyance. This scenario of imperfection might cause you to regret over making the decision to marry your spouse.

Get Complacent

Some people don't have the will to get annoyed or the strength to mull over regrets when it comes to the decision that they made. So instead of spending their energies meditating on the offence or the regret, they just get complacent. Their usual line goes like this, *"Oh, boy. Not again. I can do nothing about it. Perhaps, it's better to leave it as it is."*

However, the problem with getting complacent and accepting everything at face value is that it stops you and your spouse to grow and become better versions of yourselves. When you accept every imperfections that comes in your marriage, and just gloss over it, a time will come when every negative emotions will explode and the result might be more damaging compared to dealing with it the first time you encounter those flaws.

Deal Wisely

I have devoted the last portion of this chapter to discussing the right way of dealing with imperfections. For now, it will suffice to say that accepting the imperfections is not enough. You must also learn to deal with it wisely by doing your best to improve on it, to tolerate it, or to celebrate it as part of your uniqueness as an individual.

These responses are not conclusive. By looking deeply at your experiences, perhaps you see another way to respond to imperfections and flaws by your spouse and your marital relationship as a whole. No matter what method you use or the way you respond to those deficiencies in relationship, I hope that you would deal with it in a way that will get you closer with your spouse and deepen the intimacy inside the relationship. Each response has its own consequence. And though you are free to choose the response that you prefer to address these kinds of issues, you are not free from the consequences of the choices that you made.

Fundamental Truths about Imperfections in Marriage

Before you learn the right way of dealing with imperfections in marital relationship, it is important that you believe the fundamental truths about flaws and imperfections in marriage. These basic concepts are instrumental to help you to set the right level of expectations in marriage and thus create a room or allowance for any shortcomings that might come along the way.

There is no perfect person

We all heard the saying that *"Nobody is perfect."* And there is a lot of truth about that. No person on this planet – no matter how beautiful, how rich, and how intelligent he or she is – can be considered perfect. Thus, every person is flawed. However, the problem with most people in marriage is they expect their spouse to be perfect. They have unrealistic expectation about the way their spouse thinks, talks, and acts.

In the early stages of romantic relationship, where everything is still being filtered with rose glasses, those flaws seem inconsequential. In fact, there are some people who find it cute that their partners have these quirks and other peculiarities. Then, after the intoxicating emotions have waned, these quirks and peculiarities become the object of annoyance. If you have been this kind of person who sets the expectation too high, then you need to go back to that fundamental truth that nobody is perfect. Everyone makes mistakes and that includes your partner.

There is no perfect person for you

One dangerous tendency of people who are setting the bar too high is to think that because their partner does not measure up to the ideals that they have set in their mind, perhaps he or she is not the perfect person for them. It is in accordance with one of the most common myths that surround the idea of romantic love – the idea of perfect soulmate. According to this notion, there is a perfect person that is reserved for you. This person is the one who will make you happy and will give you the kind of love that you are looking for. You are made for each other and no other person can give you the same kind of gladness other than him or her.

I firmly believe that this idea is a false. Think about it; if there is only one perfect person for each one of us, then one mistake will destroy the whole system and will result to a chain of events that everyone will get the wrong person for them. Thus, to think that her flaws make her the wrong person for you is both false and egotistic. Do you think you are perfect? Are you free of any flaws and mistakes? That is the fundamental truth and you need to accept it. Therefore, the mistakes and imperfections of your spouse does not equate with him or her being the wrong person. What you need to change is the way your mind works.

There is no perfect marriage

Have you experienced this before? You are browsing the social media and you see posts and photos of your friends and their spouses eating dinner happily, or they are in a vacation and enjoying the beach together, or perhaps it's just a wacky picture that displays how they are happy in each other's company. Then you say to yourself, *"Good for them. They have a perfect marriage. And here I am, stuck with this person, who doesn't even know how to prepare a proper meal."* And before you know it, you are wallowing in self-pity, despising every minute that you spend with your spouse, and thinking, *"Why can't our marriage be perfect too?"*

Now, there are several issues here that you need to see more clearly, but let me focus on the more obvious. First, your friend's post in social media is merely a highlight of their marriage. In short, it doesn't represent everything that is going on in their relationship. They might seem perfect because all you see in their posts are pictures filled with smile, gladness and sweetness. But how about those times that they are not talking to each other because of what the husband said to his wife? Or what about that particular moment that they yelled to each other because no one prepared dinner? You normally don't see those moments because they are not meant to be shown in the social media. As Pastor Steven Furtick puts it, *"One of the reasons we struggle with insecurity is because we compare our behind-the-scenes with other people's highlight reel."*

"No spouse is perfect in marriage" Chindah Chindah

These are fundamental truths about imperfections and flaws in marriage. And the sooner you understand and accept these truths, the easier it would be to respond correctly to any mistakes and shortcomings that might come along the way. It will also help you in setting the level of expectation that will help you and your spouse to be free from the burden of trying to be perfect and trying to be the ideal person that each of you have created in your minds.

The Art of Acceptance and Tolerance

Though most expectations in marriage are considered too idealistic, it is still a critical aspect of marital relationship. Besides, how can you know if you are operating within the remit of your goals if you don't set any ideals for your marriage? How can you know what is good and what is bad if you don't understand what each partner expects from each other and the relationship as a whole? Setting expectations is essential, but you need to do it in the right way in order to be fully satisfied in marriage.

Another aspect that you must understand is how you can properly deal with the issue of having unmet expectations in your relationship. How does a person respond when her partner does not measure up to the ideals that she has set for her spouse? I have outlined to you the wrong response which is to get offended, wallow in regret and just get complacent on the face of these flaws and you must avoid these ways of responding to the situation at all costs. Now, here are some suggestions that you might consider when dealing with imperfections and flaws in your partner and in the marriage as a whole.

Accept your spouse for who he is – warts and all

Who doesn't want to have a partner that is selfless, thoughtful and caring? Who doesn't want to be married to a person who has a great body and physical appearance? Who doesn't want to spend their lives with someone they admire or someone who they consider their *dream boy* or *dream girl?* Whether we admit it or not, all of us have been influenced by what the media feed us about the idea of a perfect relationship. And because of these influences, we tend to shape our spouse to the image of the ideal partner that we have in mind.

Thomas Bradbury, a UCLA psychologist wisely commented, *"You don't have a line-item veto when it comes to your partner. It's a package deal; the bad comes with the good."* When it comes to marriage, there is a high possibility that your expectation towards your spouse won't be met. Don't be surprised at this. Instead, you must learn to understand the art of accepting your partner for who he is. It is not wise to reject him just because he can't measure up to the ideals that you have set for him. Acceptance is one of the essence of true love and it is important that you practise this when reality doesn't meet expectations.

Find opportunities for growth

There are aspects and facets of our being that can be considered flawed or incomplete. And some of these areas stay with us for life. In fact, I would go far as to say that these areas are meant to remain unchanged because it's part of us. Our temperaments and personalities are examples of these things. If you have been wired to become an introverted melancholic, then no one can expect you to just show up one day and be the life of the party. On the other hand, if you are a dominant choleric, then you will always have something to say when it comes to the aspect of leadership. These things stay with you – even if other people look at it as imperfections.

However, there are things in your life that can be changed and must be changed in order for yourself to be better as well as your marital relationship. These can be considered as opportunities for growth. Though, it is important to accept your partner for who he is, it is also not right to leave him as he is especially if some aspects of his being is affecting him in a negative way. Some of these areas are in the aspect of character, skills and habits.

For instance, if your spouse has the tendency to lose his temper in the middle of any conversation, yell at you and call you names, then it is a flaw in his character. You are not just to sit back and watch him as he wreak havoc in your home because your whole family will be affected by this kind of attitude. You can talk about it during his calm moments and lovingly advise him to adjust and improve his bad attitude. Another example would be your spouse's unwillingness to do the household chores. If you are doing your part to clean the house while he is just sitting on the couch and watching TV, then this might not sit well with you eventually. It's a flaw in his habits and thus must be addressed accordingly.

Confronting these kinds of flaws, mistakes and imperfections of your spouse doesn't mean that you don't love him enough and you want to change him into another person. It only means that you love him enough not to leave him where he is right now because you know that he can be better. However, let me leave an important note that if ever you decide to talk with your spouse regarding this, you must do the discuss it with him in a way that is encouraging and uplifting. Check your motives. The Bible said in Proverbs 27:5, *"Open rebuke is better than hidden love."* Let your confrontation be a display of your love for your spouse and all will go well with you.

Be Self-Responsible

Another great way to deal with imperfections in your marriage is to become self-responsible. It means that you will avoid pointing fingers when it comes to solving problem in your relationship. We all have the tendency to blame others when it comes to dealing with issues in different aspects of our lives. How many times do we hear the dialogue, *"If it were not for him, this marriage will be great and satisfying." "It is her fault that I cheated. She is always too busy at work and don't have enough time for me." "I am not responsible for whatever happens to this marriage. If he chooses to leave, then that is his fault, not mine."*

Bradbury also said, *"It's too simplistic an interpretation that your partner is the one who's wrong. We tend to point our finger at the person in front of us. We're fairly crude at processing some information. We tend not to think, 'Maybe I'm not giving her what she needs.' 'Maybe he's disgruntled because I'm not opening up to him.' Or, 'Maybe he's struggling in his relationship with other people.' The more sophisticated question is, 'In what ways are we failing to make the other partner happy?"*

The problem with blaming others for our misfortunes is that we always pitch ourselves as the victim. However, as we remove the responsibility from our hands, we also imperceptibly remove the power to solve these problems and deal with any issues directly related with it. Being self-responsible is seeing the issue with an objective frame of mind. It is all about understanding that whatever happens to your relationship is the sum total of the decisions that you and your spouse make. And you can't blame the other partner for whatever happens to you.

But what if the other person is really the one who started the issue? What if your spouse is truly the one at fault and you just responded in a way that is expected because of what he did? Are you wrong for getting mad and resenting your spouse for the way she made you feel? Let me answer this question by saying this: *You are responsible for what happens inside you. And no other persone can allow you to get hurt over and over again other than yourself.* Yes, the words and actions of your spouse might hurt a lot, but you still hold the decision to forgive him and to give him another chance. Also, you still has the choice on what improvements and adjustments you can make to avoid those things happening again. You have the capacity and you have the choice and that should be enough reasons for you to become self-responsible about your marriage.

Let Love run its course

Imperfections and flaws can cast a great shadow of doubt as to whether the relationship that you have is worth keeping or should just be ended right away. However, love – the true kind of love – can be a bright light to remove all those shadows and help you to see the good in your spouse instead of focusing on the bad. One of the definitions of love that I believe captures the essence of what true love really means is found in the Bible. It is the famous verses of Apostle Paul written in 1 Corinthians 13. Here's what it said:

Love is patient, love is kind. It does not envy, it does not boast, it is not proud. It does not dishonor others, it is not self-seeking, it is not easily angered, it keeps no record of wrongs. Love does not delight in evil but rejoices with the truth. It always protects, always trusts, always hopes, always perseveres. (1 Corinthians 13:4 – 7 NIV)

One of the best ways to show how much you love your spouse is by expressing this kind of love to him. When you try to be patient even if he fails a lot of time, you are showing him your love. When you are not proud even if you know that you are a lot better in cooking than your husband, you are displaying your love. When you grit your teeth and refuse to get angry even if she still doesn't understand your point, it is you showing your love. And when you forgive and hold no record of wrongs, then you are saying to him, *"I love you."*

When you let love run its course in your marital relationship, the darkness of mistakes and imperfections will pale in comparison in its brightness. Indeed, you are not perfect; both of you have the tendency to hurt each other even when you don't mean it, but those things won't prevent you to experience true love. Those flaws and failures might hurt, but it won't be enough to remove the light of your relationship. And that is the beauty of the art of acceptance and tolerance.

Make Room for Imperfections

Imagine your marriage as a house with a lot of rooms. Upon entering the house, you were greeted by the gorgeous living room that is painted with bright shades of red. It is adorned with pictures of your moments together. It was beautiful and it truly represents the affection and intimacy that you have for each other. Walking a little further, you can see the kitchen along with the dining room where you do a lot of things together. You cook together, wash the dishes, and of course, eat those hearty meals with each other. It was also beautiful, and not to mention, it is a place where your bond gets stronger.

You walk the stair case leading up to the second floor. The walls on the side of the stairs are filled with pictures that show how you have stayed together and helped each other during times of hardships. And o boy, you had a lot of trials and because of helping each other; you were able to go to the next level of your relationship – higher and higher. Upon reaching the second floor, you immediately noticed the master's bedroom. It's dark and was only lit by a small lamp shade. But the aroma of the room was sinking through your nerves and not to mention that it's quite hot in that room. You remember how you shared in the intimacy of sex and drew closer together by the beauty of making love. Then, there's another room beside it. That was the kid's room. And indeed, you have a lot of memories on that room as well.

Your house is a testament of your love for each other. But something was missing. And it was too late before you knew it was missing. In spite of the great beauty of your house, you noticed that it smelled really bad. The floor was dripping wet and the corners became shelter for flies and maggots. And then it hit you. You forgot to make another room – a room that is known by many names: rest room, comfort room, the toilet room. That is a flawed analogy, I know. However, it communicates to us an important lesson: every marriage, no matter how great its start is, won't keep its beauty unless a room for imperfections is made.

In your marriage, flaws and deficiencies will come your way. Some of these things must be flushed out to protect the sanctity and the beauty of your marriage. Like any other things, mistakes are bound to come in your relationship; thus you need to be prepared for it. Learn how to deal with those things in the right manner and you can also be guaranteed of the marital satisfaction that both of you will experience.

Reflection Questions:

This portion of each chapter aims to help you and your spouse to properly evaluate the principles and concepts that you have learned. Try to answer all the questions truthfully. Discuss it with your spouse so you can gain a greater insight when it comes to your partner's ideas and personal thoughts. It will also be helpful if you could share your answers with another couple who might be delighted to go in the journey with you.

1. On a scale of 1 to 10, where 10 is the highest and 1 is the lowest, how high was your expectation for your spouse and for your marriage? Do you believe that your expectation towards your relationship affects the satisfaction that you get from it? In your own assessment, is your spouse or the marriage as a whole meeting the expectations that you have set for yourself? Identify specific instances and examples that formed the basis of your opinion about expectation and reality.

_____

_____

_____

2. Consider the following statements and choose what best describes you:

   - I usually believe that successful marriage is a marriage where there are few problems to solve and fewer mistakes committed because both spouse love each other deeply and each partner doesn't want to hurt the other.

   - I am aware that problems and trials are part of any relationship. Marriage is not an exception. There will always be some form of flaws and imperfections and I am not surprised by it at all.

   Try to select the answer that genuinely communicates your view. Why do you think this is your view when it comes to marriage? Does your view of imperfections and flaws in the marital relationship help your marriage to get better or only makes matters worse

_____

_____

_____

3. How do you usually deal with imperfections, flaws and mistakes that your spouse commit? Do you usually get offended and harbour resentment towards him? Are you sometimes struggling with thoughts of regrets of marrying the person that you are with right now? Or do you adopt a complacent mindset thinking that there is no other way to improve the situation so you might as well accept it for what it is? Do you have any other response to those things that you can think about? Now, try to evaluate whether your approach in dealing with imperfections, flaws and mistakes is hindering the growth of your marriage or is helping you to become both better as a person.

_____

_____

_____

4. We have discussed the fundamental truths about imperfections in marriage. Do you believe in those fundamental truths that there is no perfect person, no perfect person for you, neither a perfect marriage, so to speak? The best way to test your answer is to look back at your response every time that you come face to face with the flaws in your spouse and your marriage as a whole.

_____

_____

_____

5. Try to answer these questions truthfully, test your answers in light of what you have done and how you responded in the

past, and if there is anything that you think needs improvement, devise a plan or strategy in order to follow through it.

- Do you accept your spouse for who he or she is – warts and all? *To answer this, evaluate if you have harboured any form of resentment, feel any kind of regret over marrying your spouse, or just plain gratitude that you married your partner.*
- Do you usually find opportunities for growth when it comes to those aspects of imperfections that are meant to be improved?
- Do you take responsibility for whatever happens in your relationship, not putting the entire blame on your spouse, rather finding reasons why it happened in the first place and if you have a part in it?
- Are you allowing love to run its course? Are you allowing love to be the primary motivation in being intimate with your spouse in spite of the imperfections that you are witnessing in him everyday?

_____

_____

_____

FOURTH CRITERION:
THE POWER OF COMMENDATION

CHAPTER 6

"The deepest principle in human nature
is the craving to be appreciated."

– William James

When was the last time that you received a word of encouragement from somebody? Or the last time that someone noticed your outfit, your hair, or your overall appearance, and just raved and praised you for how you look? When was the last time that somebody commended you for the quality of your work, or the way you speak in public, or just the way you handle things? Can you still remember the last time that somebody affirmed your ability and your wit, or just simply appreciate you?

Can you still remember those particular moments? I bet that you still recall those moments because that would qualify as one of the best moments of your life, right? And I would also bet that you won't forget the people who went out of their way just to appreciate you for who you are and what you do. Praise, commendation, appreciation, affirmation – it goes with a lot of names, but it speaks of only one thing. You matter. You are worth something.

Mark Twain famously said, *"I can live for two months on a good compliment."* Well, we all know that he was just exaggerating, but his statement speaks of an essential truth and principle in the arena of human relations. Commendation, compliment and appreciation are crucial to having a satisfying and fulfilled life. Without it, life loses its value, your self-esteem suffers, and you question whether you still have something to live for that is actually worth living for. Appreciation is important. As Mother Teresa puts it, *"People crave attention and appreciation more than they do bread."*

If appreciation is important to all people, then your spouse won't be an exception. At the same time, the quality of your marriage will be directly affected by the quality and the frequency of the compliments, affirmations, and words of encouragement that you give to each other. If you have been with your spouse for a couple of years now, then you know how difficult it is to live together without speaking words of affirmation to each other. It's hard to live with another person who only speaks negative things about you. It's a nightmare to be with somebody, whose goal in life is to point out all your mistakes, criticizing your flaws and shortcomings, and give you negative feedback on everything that you do.

Therefore, it is essential for any married couples to understand this fourth criterion, which is the power of commendation. That is what this chapter is all about. First, we will go in detail about the definition of commendation and the different fundamental principles that you must know about it. Next, we will elaborate on the importance of commendation and the different benefits that you can reap if you and your spouse will do your best to go out of your way to appreciate each other. Lastly, I will share with you some tips that you can implement right away in order to take advantage of the power of commending each other.

Defining Commendation

The word *"Commend"* came from the Latin word *"Commendare"* which means to commit and to entrust. It evokes an image of a funeral service where people *commit* and *entrust* the person's soul in the hands of God. To elaborate, to commend someone is to believe in the person's ability or capacity to deliver. People entrust the dead man's soul to God because they believe that God is the only one who has the power to determine where the soul of the dead person will go.

In our language today, to commend someone means to praise, appreciate, or approve a person because of his ability, wisdom, or any other desirable trait. Merriam Webster dictionary defines the word *"Commendation"* as *"the act of praising or approving something."* It is all about appreciating the value and worth of a person. When you are commending someone, it means that you are seeing the good things about that person whether it is his or her physical appearance, wit, or ability.

Commendation is an essential part of any relationship, and most importantly in marriage. We need to have an extensive understanding of the concept and principles surrounding commendation because it will help you to determine whether you and your spouse will enjoy the company of each other or you will live a miserable life together.

Basic Principles of Commendation

Commending another person affects a lot of aspects of his being including his self-image, self-esteem, self-worth, and even his perspective on what he can or what he can't do. We hold an enormous power in our hands and that power can help other people in unleashing the best within them. It is therefore a wonder why most of us are not utilising the power that is available to us.

In the last chapter, we discussed about the reality of imperfections and flaws about you, your spouse and the marriage as a whole. We recognised that those things are necessary parts of your relationship and there are some flaws that you can work on and improve. To help you in improving those areas, you can employ the power of appreciation. And these are the basic principles that you need to remember:

Be liberal with praise

In his best-selling book, *"How to Win Friends and Influence People,"* the author Dale Carnegie said, *"Be hearty in your approbation and lavish in your praise."* If there is one resource that we need to use over and over again, it is our resource of appreciation for other people, especially our spouse. Think about it. You chose to marry your spouse for myriads of reasons. And if you are like most couples, then I believe that one of those reasons is because you genuinely like a lot of things about your spouse. Perhaps, it is her appearance that you can't help but just stare at her for hours. Or maybe it's because of his ability to lead other people and encourage them to become better version of themselves. Or maybe you liked her because of her ability to sing, to dance, to cook, and a lot more qualities that you genuinely appreciate.

During the early days of romantic relationship, couples tend to zero in on those qualities that they like about their partner. The guy can't help but to gush out how beautiful his woman is and he just bragged about her in front of their friends. On the other hand, the woman can't stop talking about how caring his man is. As one of the most cliché lines of lovers say, *"There's no other like him!"* And because of the abundance of praise and appreciation, both of them feel good about themselves, their self-images improve and they believe that they can do more. As studies have already determined, positive feedback increases the likelihood of betterment for a person.

However, as the relationship gets older, most couples also decrease their appreciation and commendation to one another. And sadly, the kind words of encouragement and affirmation are being replaced with critical feedbacks and sarcastic remarks. And before they know it, both of them doubt themselves and doubt the relationship as well. That is why it is important to be liberal in your praise to your spouse. You don't always have to wait for something spectacular to happen just to compliment your spouse. All you need is a keen eye to see something that you like and immediately utter your appreciation about it.

Do you like the way he dons that black suit? Say it. Do you appreciate that she took the time to make you coffee and breakfast ? Tell it to her. Do you feel loved because he brought you flowers? Gush about it! Whatever you like and whatever makes you feel good, say it to your spouse. Be liberal in your praise.

Be Genuine in your appreciation

As much as you should be generous in telling good things, you must also check your motives to make sure that what you are saying comes really from your heart. Your spouse can smell it, if you are just using those compliments to gain favour from her or you just want to receive something in return. The best compliments are those that are done with a genuine motivation to praise and not expecting to receive anything in return.

Dale Carnegie recounts one incident that shows the beauty of genuine appreciation and its power to increase the self-esteem and confidence of that person. Here's the story in his own words:

I was waiting in line to register a letter in the post office at Thirty-third Street and Eight Avenue in New York. I noticed that the registry clerk was bored with his job – weighing envelopes, handing out stamps, making change, issuing receipts – the same monotonous grind year after year. So I said to myself: *"I am going to try to make that chap like me. Obviously, to make him like me, I must say something nice, not about myself, but about him."*

So I asked myself, *"What is there about him that I can honestly admire?"* That is sometimes a hard question to answer especially with strangers; but in this case, it happened to be easy. I instantly saw something I admired to no end.

So while he was weighing my envelope, I remarked with enthusiasm: *"I certainly wish I had your head of hair."*

He looked up, half-startled, his face beaming with smiles. *"Well, it isn't as good as it used to be,"* he said modestly. I assured him that although it might have lost some of its pristine glory, nevertheless it was still magnificent. He was immensely pleased. We carried on a pleasant conversation and the last thing he said to me was: *"Many people have admired my hair."*

I told this story once in public; and a man asked me afterwards: *"What did you want to get out of him?"*

What was I trying to get out of him!!! What was I trying to get out of him!!!

If we are so contemptibly selfish that we can't radiate a little happiness and pass on a bit of honest appreciation without trying to screw something out of the other person in return . . . we shall meet with the failure we so richly deserve.

Oh yes, I did want something out of that chap. I wanted something priceless. And I got it. I got the feeling that I had done something for him without his being able to do anything whatever in return for me. That is a feeling that glows and sings in your memory long after the incident has passed.

Imagine employing the same scenario with your spouse. Instead of focusing on finding faults, you are always trying to see what's good about her. You gloss over her flaws but instead you affirm her good qualities, then you celebrate together. In fact, I believe trying to find something to appreciate about your spouse can be a piece of cake. Well, you know her better than most people so you know those qualities that truly make her shine. Talk a lot about those things.

Praise in public

Do you want to magnify the power of appreciation by ten-folds? Then you just need to do it in front of other people. Praise your spouse when you are with your friends. In fact, you can do better by talking about him when he is not around. Let your family and friends know how good a husband he is, how much he respects you, and how well provided your family is because of his efforts. And when those people that you talk to about your husband extend the compliment to your spouse, then the power of appreciation will be magnified.

There is no feeling like being praised in front of other people. That's why there are some networking groups who are employing these techniques to get new recruits. They will talk to one another with the people that they invited and say the following lines, *"I admire this guy because..."* as he talks about all the good things that they know about that person. And when the person feels appreciated, what will he do? Most likely, he will come back for more and will join the marketing group.

In the same way, your marriage will benefit if you will both go out of your way to lavish praise on your spouse in public. Brag about the great qualities of your spouse to your parents. Share how awesome your wife's cooking is to your friends. Talk about your husband's accomplishment at work to your officemates. And as you appreciate one another in front of other people, your intimacy will grow as well as the desire to do more good things to each other.

As a side note, let me say that as much as I am encouraging you to praise your spouse in public, you must also remember the other side of the coin, which is to criticise him only in private. Never shout to the world the flaws and imperfections of your spouse. Remember, you are in partnership with each other and as partners; you must both protect the welfare of union. If you have been hurt by the action of your spouse and you need someone to talk to, don't talk to a lot of people. Talk to a friend that you are accountable to. In that way, you are protecting the reputation of your spouse while at the same time doing what you can do to weather the storm.

Commend based on needs and perception

Man and woman have different needs and perceptions when it comes to appreciation and affirmation. Men strongly feel the need to feel significant in terms of the things that he is toiling for. He wants to know that his efforts are not in vain and he is doing a good job in whatever he does. Women, on the other hand, are more inclined to feel significant when their feelings are being validated and when they are secured by the love of their spouse. Therefore, it is important to commend your spouse depending on the things that he or she needs to hear.

Also, it would be wise to practice appreciation based on the love language of your spouse. We have discussed the concept of love language in Chapter 3 so I won't elaborate it here, but what I want to tell you is that you should speak your commendation based on each other's love language. For instance, if your wife's love language is acts of service, then you can speak to her your admiration and explain that because you appreciate her, you will do the dishes tonight. Another example would be a husband with the love language of physical touch. Try to hold his hand, embrace him or give him a quick kiss on the lips and say how much you admire all that he is doing for the family. Combining the power of commendation with the principle of love language will multiply it's effect by ten-folds.

The Importance of Commendation

The power of appreciation and affirmation has been analysed by various professionals who are working in the area of human relations. And over and over again, the results of their studies reveal its importance in interpersonal relationships. Commendation takes on another level of importance when it comes to married couples where words are one of the most important currencies that are used. If you want to improve your relationship with your spouse, increase her self-esteem and self-confidence, or just bring out the best from your partner, then you can't ignore the principle of commendation. Here are some of the most notable benefits of appreciating your spouse.

Commendation will satisfy the cravings of both of you

Think about this scenario. Your spouse is undergoing a tremendous challenge at work. The economy is in a recession and a lot of people are getting laid off from their jobs. Your spouse's position is also being threatened, thus he feels so stressed and pressured. He has spread negative emotions to his work and so can't provide the excellent and quality service that are expected of him by his manager. He is doing his best, but it seems that all that his manager can see are the deficiencies in his performance.

Every time that he comes home after working for a whole day, he will spend the entire night watching TV and seem entirely oblivious of your own need as his wife. Therefore, you always get mad at him. He still brings the money that you need for the day to day expenses of your family, but you can't see it nor appreciate his effort. All you can see is an insensible husband who does nothing but to watch TV. So what do you do? You nag him and pester him about all your needs that he is not meeting. And what do you receive? Nothing. You don't know if he's just too tired to argue, or he just doesn't care anymore.

But you are blinded by the truth that all he needs right now is some form of encouragement, kind words that will be uttered by the person who he expects to hear it from; to be appreciated and affirmed that indeed, he is a man worthy of such praise. So instead of nagging and criticising him, why not give him something that he really craves right now? Think about saying that he is a good provider, that he is a warrior who can conquer all his challenges, that he is a guy who you truly admire because you know the greatness inside him. Can you imagine what it will do to your relationship and to him as a person?

Commendation will refresh the relationship

Marriage is sometimes full of challenges and a lot of things that will truly test your capacity and ability to withstand. There are times when the pressure and stress of married life might catch up with both of you and will tend to force you to say things that you know will just hurt the relationship. However, when you make it a practice to say those words of affirmation, appreciation and commendation to each other, then you can refresh the relationship.

A 10-year study was carried out by researchers from the University of Washington where they followed the lives of 95 couples who are just starting in their marriages. During their study, the researchers discovered an interesting finding and this result enables them to predict with 87% accuracy which of those couples will end up in divorce. And what is the criterion that they used? It's the way the couples talk about each other to their families, friends, and even strangers. The researchers concluded that when a spouse speaks in encouraging and glowing terms about his or her partner, they are a candidate to a lasting marriage. On the other hand, those couples who talk with cynicism about each other eventually end up in divorce.

The research only shows how important it is to speak encouraging words about each other as well as to see one another in a more positive light. Indeed, we all have our flaws and imperfections. And most of the time, couples are being driven by their own selfish motives. However, if both of the couples will focus and zero in on the qualities of their spouse that highlight what is good, then they can experience the continuous refreshment in the relationship no matter how long they have been together already.

Commendation will boost self-esteem and self-confidence

Dr. Suzanne Phillips, a psychologist, said that low self-esteem is a relationship killer. Having this problem is dangerous because a spouse who has a low self-esteem will be prone to doubt himself as well as the love of his partner for him. It also lowers the expectations of what you should receive in the relationship, which speaks of the lowering of self-worth. In addition to this, low self-esteem can also affect your communication and way of dealing with conflicts in a negative manner. Thus, it is essential that each spouse finds ways to boost each other's self-esteem and confidence.

When we are being seen by other people in a positive light, the doubts that we have about ourselves slowly vanishes. In the same vein, when someone is appreciating us and always talk about the good things they see in us, we tend to believe them and thus see ourselves in a better light. Considering these realisations, it is of utmost importance that you make it a point to speak those words of encouragement, appreciation and admiration to your spouse.

Commendation draws out the best in you

A study was conducted by Emily Heaphy and Marcial Losada to understand the effectiveness of positive feedback in the performance of employees. To make it even more difficult, the positive feedback is compared with a ratio to the negative feedback that the employee receives in order to find out the right ratio that will maximise the effectiveness of the feedback system. The interesting finding that they discover is that only positive feedback can motivate an employee to continue on his level of performance and exert the same effort, vigour and determination to do his job. On the other hand, negative feedback has not been useful to encourage people to put their best efforts.

The same thing has been noted in a research conducted by John Gottman, a psychologist, where he tried to analyse the likelihood of a couple going through divorce by looking at the ratio of positive to negative comments to one another. He ascertained that a healthy ratio of positive and negative feedbacks for married couples should be 5:1. In short, in every single critical or negative remark, there must be five positive affirmation and encouraging words.

The results of both of these studies speak of the importance of positive affirmation and commendation in the dynamics of human relationship, whether it is work related or in the setup of marriage. No one can thrive on receiving negative feedbacks and what it only does is to limit the performance as well as prove to the person who criticises that he or she is indeed right. On the contrary, speaking words of praise and appreciation to another person enables him or her to sustain the level of performance that he or she has attained and in most cases, make the person believe that he is capable of more things. In short, commendation will truly help in drawing out the best in you and your spouse.

No one can deny the importance of commendation. And even if we remove the results of these studies, we all know for a fact that a genuine, positive compliment can bring you a long way from where you are right now. It is essential. It is important. It is crucial. And if you are to learn the skills needed to create a satisfying marriage, then put commendation and appreciation on the top of your list.

3 Ways to Commend Each Other

Commendation is essential to help a person to become a better version of himself. In the context of marriage, appreciation and affirmation helps each spouse to boost their self-esteem and cultivate a healthier self-image. Approval also deepens the security that they have with regards to each other's love and affection. And more than what it does to each individual spouse, commendation also strengthen the very foundation of the institution of marriage. Now, what's left is for you to learn some tips and insights of how you can commend each other, build each other up and make it a habit that will increase the likelihood of having a lasting marriage. Consider these tips and I encourage you to apply it right away.

Appreciate each other's hard work

As married couples, husband and wife are both expected to work in making the relationship better and thriving. However, with individual personalities, perspective and beliefs, it is not uncommon to see them working in different directions. The husband might perceive the meaning of working hard as spending a lot of time at work and grinding until night just to make sure that he climbs up the corporate ladder. On the other hand, the wife might work hard by finishing her job on time and make sure that she can spend more time with the family at night.

''It doesn't hurt to appreciate your spouse in everything he or she does for the family'' Chindah Chindah

As you can see, both of them are working hard for the relationship to thrive. However, the problem is that they have different perception of the meaning of hard work for the family. And these differences in the way they see things might be a cause for conflict in the future. The wife might say, *"Hey! Can't you see my effort to finish all my tasks during the day so we can spend more time in the night? Why are you always coming home late?"* To which the husband might respond like this, *"Come on! You can't be serious! I'm grinding my body just to make sure that we can pay the bills and put food on the table! Can't you appreciate my hard work?"*

Both of them are coming from their sincere desire to work hard for their family, but because they are both seeing it in their own perspective, a conflict was created. The best way to solve this is to talk and explain each other's perspective when it comes to hard work. After that, don't forget to appreciate and compliment your spouse for the effort that he or she is exerting for the family and for the relationship. And perhaps, you can arrive at a compromise. The husband can reduce his time at work, while the wife can find other opportunities to make money that she can do during her free time. No matter what resolution you might come up with, just remember to always appreciate each other's hard work.

Support each other's dream

We all heard the saying, *"If you truly love the person, you've got to set them free."* In the context of what we are talking about, it is supporting the ambition or the dream of your partner. Most people have it. Some have acquired that dream since they were still young and they have live all their lives just to achieve it. Others only had that dream later in life. But the problem is that there are times where people see their marriage as an obstacle for them to achieve their dreams.

"Who will pay the bills?" *"Who will send my children to school?"* *"What if I will lose my precious time with my family?"* It could be a tricky situation, and therefore, a lot of dreamers just quit their dreams for their family. Who can judge them? No one. They just do what they think is best. But if you can handle the risk, then I would challenge you to support each other's dream.

I remember the famous story of Robert Manry and his brave voyage to cross the Atlantic Ocean. Manry was working as a copy editor for the Cleveland *Plain Dealer* for 10 years. He eventually became bored at his job and decided that he wanted to do something different. So he had bought the materials that he needed and began his plans to cross the Atlantic Ocean and go to England with his boat, *Tinkerbelle.* It was the smallest boat to make the voyage with a size of 13 ½ feet. Then on May 24, 1965, he started his journey out of the dock of Falmouth, Massachusetts towards the open ocean.

He did not tell a lot of people about his plans for fear that they will discourage him to do it. Without any assurance that he could make it out alive, he wrote to some of his relatives to which his sister wrote back: *"It is wonderful to see someone carry out his dream. So few of us take a chance."* But the person who gave

Manry his biggest support was no other than his wife, Virginia. He said later on, *"No one in the world has as a wonderful wife as I. Virginia could have insisted that I behave as other rational men did and give up this 'crazy voyage.' But she knew that I was stepping to the music of a different drummer and she granted me the invaluable book of self-realization by allowing me to keep pace with the music I heard."*

The journey of Manry was perilous and life-threatening. His boat was too small for the voyage and the ocean that he needed to cross was full of large ships and freighters that could destroy his vessel without warning. He was alone for weeks and the loneliness that he felt caused him to hallucinate. The food became tasteless. His rudder broke three times. He faced storms that swept him overboard. Indeed, death starred him in the face. But after 78 days he reached England.

Manry never expected the welcoming party. There were three hundred vessels that escorted him into the marina and 40,000 people who were waiting on the shore for him. His voyage has inspired a lot of people and he became a hero. And there in the shore, waiting for him, was the hero of his life, Virginia. If there was a quality that Virginia has, it was her ability to support her husband to pursue his dreams. Of course, not everyone would be comfortable knowing that their spouse is risking their lives somewhere. I could just imagine the sleepless nights that Virginia also experienced and all she could do is to pray and entrust her husband to God.

Having the support of your spouse is one of the greatest forms of commendation that an individual can receive. There might be times in a couple's life that a spouse will have a unique project in mind, something that is out of the ordinary activities that you usually enjoy together. During these moments, you have two options. You can either stop him in pursuing his dream or give him your full support. I encourage you to wisely consider all the possibilities that can happen. And after that, you decide.

Celebrate each other's progress

One of the most common mistakes of couples is to wait for something major to happen before they commend and express their appreciation and admiration to their spouse. They usually feel that words of affirmation must be very special so it should only be reserved for those moments of extreme importance like when they have already paid the house in full, or sold their product to their very first customer, or upon accepting a promotion at the office. However, this perspective goes against one of the fundamental principles of commendation which is to be liberal in praise.

This mindset of waiting for that huge event before they celebrate comes hand in hand with the mindset that celebration must always be big and expensive. And since couples don't want to spend any unnecessary expenses, they just wait for that huge success to come before they call a celebration. But instead of waiting for that huge event to happen, why not celebrate milestones and progress along the way? Celebrate when you have made the down payment for the house. Celebrate every major step that you are doing in your business like creating a website. Also, you don't have to be expensive in celebrating. A simple dinner will do. Or perhaps treat your wife with ice cream on the street along the way home.

Celebrating each other's progress will help you to be more determined in achieving the next milestone and the ultimate goal that you are aiming for. It also enables you to enjoy the company of each other and build you up not just as a couple, but as a team with common aspirations and dreams. And besides, who doesn't want ice cream every now and then?

The Exquisite Gift that is Free

They say that the best things in life are free. That statement rings true most of the time. While most people are trying to *buy* their own share of the gift happiness, there are individuals who are choosing a more exquisite one. And that is the free gift of appreciation. The good thing about this gift in addition to it being free, is you can also give it to other persons who might also need appreciation without ever losing it. So, I would encourage you to squander it especially if it is for your spouse. Be lavish in giving her praise.

I know at times you might feel that your spouse doesn't deserve it. Well, my friend, who does? All of us have our own share of mistakes, flaws and imperfections. And what will you lose if you will consistently shower your partner with lavish appreciation? Nothing. In fact, you have nothing to lose, but you have everything to gain.

If you sincerely desire to have a more satisfying marriage, a more loving spouse, and a happier life, then don't waste your time. Start today by writing everything that is good about your spouse. Write everything from his physical appearance, her unique talents and gifts, and even the hard work that he does for the family. Then, let your spouse know that you genuinely appreciate him. Start today. It's free. And it's one of the best gifts that you can ever give.

Reflection Questions:

This portion of each chapter aims to help you and your spouse to properly evaluate the principles and concepts that you have learned. Try to answer all the questions truthfully. Discuss it with your spouse so you can gain a greater insight when it comes to your partner's ideas and personal thoughts. It will also be helpful if you could share your answers with another couple who might be delighted to go in the journey with you.

1. On a scale of 1 to 10, where 10 is the highest and 1 is the lowest, how frequently do you commend your spouse? Do you believe that commendation, appreciation and affirmation are critical to the success of marriage? When was the last time that you received genuine words of affirmation from your partner? How does it make you feel? Does it help you to feel closer to your spouse? Why or why not?

_____

_____

_____

2. Are you inclined to praise someone because you genuinely appreciate the person or you just to gain a favour from him? In connection with being genuine, are you being liberal with your praise? Do you believe that people must do something or be something before he or she receives a commendation? What do you think is the lesson that you can glean from the story of Dale Carnegie and the Postal employee?

_____

_____

_____

3. After learning the importance of commendation in a relationship, can you give an honest opinion whether you believe it or not? Also, do you agree that people are craving for

attention and appreciation? Elaborate on your perspective on this matter. In relation to the concept of marriage, what other benefits can you think about when it comes to appreciating and affirming your spouse?

_____

_____

_____

4. I have given you three different ways that you can commend each other. Out of the three ways, what aspect are you struggling with the most? Do you and your spouse have the tendency to have a different concept of hard work that might cause conflict in the future? As for the aspect of supporting each other's dream, do you still know the dream and ambition of your spouse? Are you willing to support each other to achieve your individual dreams?

_____

_____

_____

5. Do you have the tendency to wait for a major thing to happen before you celebrate with your spouse? What do you think is your underlying reason for this kind of perspective? Do you believe in the idea that you must celebrate each other's progress no matter how small it is? Let me challenge you to celebrate today because you have reached this section of this book. Go out and have dinner. Watch a movie together. Do something different to celebrate today's progress!

_____

_____

_____

FIFTH CRITERION:
THE CORRECT WAY OF CORRECTION

CHAPTER 7

"Brevity and conciseness are the parents of correction."

– Hosea Ballou

Conflicts and disagreements are inevitable aspects of marriage. In the same way, imperfections, flaws and mistakes are bound to plague the relationship sooner or later. All these things can affect the lives of the spouses either in a positive or a negative way and that will be based on the way that they handled the conflict or correct the mistakes and shortcomings of each other.

However, for most people, correction is not really an interesting idea. Of course, there are some people who correct others like they are getting paid for it, but for a lot of individuals, just the mention of the idea that they need to confront someone and correct another person for something that he has done wrong is worth cringing. Well, who wants to be a harbinger of bad news or become the main cause of any strain in their relationship?

We all hate being corrected. We know the pain of having someone tell us to our face that we did something wrong. It hurts our ego and our pride, and if we do not handle the correction properly or the correction has been delivered in a rude and uncaring manner, then our relationship with that person will likely be negatively affected. On the other hand, we all believe that correction is necessary. Without it, we will tend to continue on the wrong path or commit a lot of mistakes in our lives. We don't want that and thus we are faced with a dilemma. On one hand, we don't want to be corrected, on the other, we all believe that correction is important.

The dilemma of correction is multiplied ten times in the lives of married couples. They are two people who swore to love and accept each other warts and all. They are willing to do anything for their relationship except to cause pain and hurt to each other. How then, will they handle the dilemma of correction? Indeed, it's a tricky topic, but it deserves to be discussed since the ability of a couple to handle conflicts including their capacity to correct and accept correction can determine the destiny of their relationship.

In this chapter, we will discuss the concept of correction and the need to do it in order for marriage to become successful. We will also look at the usual ways couples deal with mistakes while noting the side effects of each approach. Next, we will look at the different principles of correction. If correction is to be done right, then you need to do it according to timeless principles that govern human interaction. Lastly, we will look at some practical tips to apply those principles of correction in your marriage.

The Reality of Making Mistakes

We have established in the previous chapters the reality of imperfections in our lives. All people – no matter how rich he is or how great her physical qualities are – cannot be perfect. Everyone has their own flaws and imperfections. In relation to this truth, there is another reality that we need to address. And that is the reality that imperfect human beings are bound to commit mistakes in their lives.

"Correct your spouse the way you want to be corrected" Chindah Chindah

With regards to making mistakes, marriage is not an exception. No matter how much love you have for one another, there will be times that you will commit some blunders in the relationship. Some might be petty. A mistake in the ingredients that your wife used in cooking your favourite dish or simply forgetting to throw the trash outside is a common example of petty mistakes. There are also big mistakes such as investing half of your hard-earned money or your entire savings in dubious schemes in the hope of gaining more. And lastly, there are those kinds of mistakes that can end your marriage such as infidelity or physically abusing your wife.

Married couples cannot escape the reality that they are bound to make mistakes – sooner or later. There are mistakes that are more critical than the others, but all of these slipups can spark arguments, conflicts, and disagreements and thus, the need for knowledge and skills in how to handle it. Depending on the potential degree of the consequence of a mistake, there must be correction along the way. That is not to say that every mistake – no matter how small or trivial must be corrected. Wisdom must be applied in this kind of situation. Nevertheless, having the ability to correct the mistakes in the right way is a must for every married couple who aim to have a lasting marriage.

Usual Approaches in Dealing with Mistakes

As unique individuals, we have different approaches when it comes to dealing with mistakes. While some are bolder in confronting the person who committed the blunder, others are more passive and have a greater tendency to just pass off the mistake and move on. While there are a myriad ways of responding to conflict, it is crucial to understand that the way you handle those negative events could affect the marriage and determine whether it will last or it will end.

This concept has been proven by a study carry out by researchers at the Univeristy of Michigan. The goal of the study was to identify the role of conflict-handling to the stability of marriage. The researchers interviewed 373 couples for four times over a period of 16 years. They found out that some of those marriages are already headed to divorce even before they started due to the differences in their approach to handling conflicts. While one of the couples wanted to resolve the conflict, the other just wanted to ignore it and move on. The researchers concluded that the behaviour of the spouses when it comes to handling negative events could predict the longevity of their marriage.

Considering the conclusions reached of that study, we need to have a serious reflection about the approach that we use in resolving conflicts especially in confronting our partners with regards to mistakes committed. Our upbringing, experiences, and the things that we learned along the way will determine the approach that we use when we are faced with a decision to confront a mistake. Here are some of the most common approaches. Try to see if you will fall to any of these four categories of people.

The Nice Guy

We all know the nice guy. He is a guy that is loved by everybody. He smiles a lot, he is cheerful with everyone, he never argues with anyone and he is never angry. It seems that everybody wants to have a nice guy as their friends. It is great to have somebody on your side that will support all of your decisions – no matter how absurd it is. Well, he's a nice guy! What else can he do?

Some couples carry this *"Nice Guy"* approach when it comes to dealing with mistakes inside marriage. Even if their partner does them wrong or do something that is totally annoying, they just brush it off and say, *"Oh, well. That's normal."* Since they do not want to be involved in any argument, they tend to support all the decisions of their spouses even if they know deep down inside that it is the wrong choice. They also avoid getting angry. For them, being angry is bad and will only lead to unnecessary pains so they just avoid it.

However, here's the problem with the *"Nice Guy"* approach in dealing with mistakes: *Everyone gets angry. The only difference is that some people give a free vent to it, while others suppress it.* If you or your spouse seem to manifest the ideals of a *"Nice Guy"* when it comes to dealing with mistakes, then there's a big problem that is looming your way. If one of you never gets angry, always smile, and never argues, then you need to be prepared for the possibility that one day, it will explode and the damage in the relationship could be devastating.

FIFTH CRITERION: THE CORRECT WAY OF CORRECTION

The Beast

This approach is the exact opposite of the *"Nice Guy"* approach. For someone who is dealing with mistakes using the *"Beast"* approach, everything is worth the anger and the argument. For them, there are no petty or big mistakes. If there is a blunder committed, then they must get angry.

There are individuals who carry this approach in their marriage. And it is equally destructive like the *"Nice Guy"* approach. Imagine a life where every wrong that you do will be confronted with anger of your spouse. Can you live a married life where argument is in abundance because your spouse could not accept that you are an imperfect husband or wife? Or perhaps, you are the one who is approaching the mistakes of your spouse like a beast. You are not necessarily looking for the mistakes, but when you see one, you lose all control.

Though, I believe that expressing anger could be healthy in a relationship because it improves the dynamics of emotions and the marriage as a whole, I strongly argue against expressing anger over a lot of things including those seemingly petty stuffs. Think about it. If your wife forgot to add salt to your fried chicken, is it right to get mad at her? If your husband left the plate of popcorn on the table is it right to yell at him and tell him that he was wrong in doing it? As the Bible says in Proverbs 19:11, *"Sensible people control their temper; they earn respect by overlooking wrongs."*

The Martyr

This category is where a lot of people belong. Unlike the *"Beast"* where mistakes won't go unnoticed and every blunder will result to anger, the *"Martyr"* tends to overlook those mistakes. However, unlike the *"Nice Guy"* where an individual might pretend that it's alright, the *"Martyr"* can voice out his frustration from time to time, yet no actions will be taken to correct the mistake.

Martyrs thrive in their love for their spouses. They put a lot of importance in their marriage and they try their best to protect it –

no matter how much it costs. Yet, in the process of protecting the relationship by accepting the mistake and overlooking it, these individuals sacrifice their joy, their peace and their comforts. I do not mean to take light of their effort to keep the relationship. What I'm imploring here is perhaps there is a better way. An approach where you can keep the relationship while at the same time keep your dignity as well.

The Righteous Judge

A lot of people also fall into this category. As the name suggest, this approach pertains to acting like a judge when it comes to mistakes that committed by another person. They stand and wait for the next blunder and the next error, and upon committing it, they immediately point it out and criticise. In fairness to those Righteous Judges, they do not necessarily get angry. They are usually calm and composed, yet what's annoying with them is their sarcastic remarks and *holier-than-thou* attitude.

For married couples, you need to understand that you are in a relationship not to look out for each other's mistakes, rather to encourage growth. Perhaps, the motive of the Righteous Judge is admirable like she just wants everything to be perfect for their marriage. Or it could also be corrupt such as wanting to exalt himself above you, showing that he is superior in knowledge, wisdom and experience.

Have you identified the persona that you display when dealing with mistakes? I know that you might not be happy with what you have discovered right now, but trust me, knowing where you stand is essential to plotting the course to go where you need to be. You might be a suppressing nice guy, a destructive beast, a poor martyr or an annoying judge; but you don't have to be that way always. The remaining content of this chapter will help you to develop the right approach when facing with the task of correcting a mistake or confronting your spouse who blundered.

The Principles of Correction

Dr. Suzanne Phillips, a psychologist and co-author of the book,

"Healing Together: A Couple's Guide to Coping with Trauma and Post-Traumatic Stress, said, *"In my work with couples, I find that the corrections partners make of each other may be conscious or unconscious, controlling, competitive, playful, mutual or invited. They most often reflect some mix of the couple's relationship, their individual personalities, and the social context they find themselves in."*

If you are to learn the right way of handling confrontation and correction, then you can't just rely solely on your emotions, your upbringing and your experiences. All of those things have been coloured by your motives and perspectives in dealing with things in your life. You need to cultivate a more objective view and paradigm about confrontation and correcting mistakes based on sound principles and concepts. Consider the following suggestions and reflect on how you could apply them to your marriage.

The Principle of Tough Love

Some individuals might argue against the concept of correcting their spouse. They reason that if you truly love your spouse, then you will just accept him including any mistakes that he commits in the course of your relationship. However, if this logic is applied in all marital relationships, then there will be no growth in the individual personalities and characters of each spouse. If the husband will commit the mistake of buying a lot of stuff using his credit card and the wife will not step forward to correct him, then there might come a time when both of them will be broke and no one can provide for their family.

Correction is essential, but you need to understand that there is a wrong way to correct, which was discussed earlier about the different approaches in handling correction, and a right way to do it. There is a great possibility that both approaches will hurt, even if you do it the right way. However, if you will take the time to learn the skills needed to adopt the correct approach in confronting your spouse about the error that they have committed, then I can guarantee that both of you as well as your relationship will greatly benefit.

The *Principle of Tough Love* takes inspiration from one of the Proverbs in the Bible which says, *"Better is open rebuke than hidden love."* Yes, correcting your spouse might sting, and might hurt his pride, but believe me when I say that correcting him is a better display of your love than letting him go on in that mistake which concerns an important aspect of his life. However, though tough love encourages correction, it also implores us to do it with an attitude of love, respect and dignity.

In short, you don't correct your spouse because you hate what she made you feel last night. Also, you don't criticise the blunders of your wife because you believe that you are better than her. And you don't disapprove the actions of your husband in a way that is insulting and damaging such as using names and using rude comparisons and analogy. No. If you are to correct your spouse, then you must do it in the spirit of love, respect and dignity. There is no other way.

The Principle of Privacy

We all have the tendency to tell other people about the mistakes of our spouses which have impacted us badly. Perhaps, it is one of the ways to release the welling emotions inside of us or maybe it just feels good when you know that there is another person who is willing to listen to you unlike your busy partner. However, you need to understand that correcting mistakes will not succeed if you let those blunders become a public knowledge.

Think about this scenario. Your husband did not come home last night and he didn't give you any warning. He came early the next morning and you could tell that he's been up all night. There was no hint that he spent the evening drinking alcohol because he looked sober and he could talk normally. Then, you came to the only logical conclusion: *He is seeing someone and he spent the night in another woman's house.*

You got raving mad at him and you yelled at the top of your voice, *"How can you do this to me? I did everything for you and yet this is what you returned for my love! I hate you!"* Then you angrily paced towards the kitchen, took the car key, bolted out of the door and drove off without looking back to your husband. You didn't know what to do. All you could think was how much you hated your husband for being unfaithful to you. Then you went to the first person that came into your mind – your best friend. She can help you. Though, she did not give you her 100% support in marrying your husband, you knew that she would still help you especially during this time.

So you went to her house and cried for three hours on her shoulder. She asked you, *"What's wrong my dear?"* And you go on raving about what your husband did to you while including frequent references of some moments when you became suspicious and you thought, *"Now, everything is clear to me."* Your friend was sad and delighted at the same time. She called some of your friends and you had your girl's conference picking up on the bad qualities of your husband. Oh, you were destroying him through your conversations.

Now, what if you are wrong? What if your husband was too tired at work that he did not notice the time and fell asleep? I know that might be an exaggeration, but let me drive the point home. When you talk about your spouse's mistake to any third party, you are destroying him in front of other people without giving him the chance to redeem himself. Is that what you want to do? Maybe not. But the implications of your action of taking those mistakes in public might still be permanently damaging for your spouse.

The *Principle of Privacy* simply states that you should never correct the mistakes of your spouse out in the open. You should do it in private where no one but the two of you will talk. By employing the principle of privacy, you are showing your respect to your partner as well as the genuine care that you have for his or her welfare. Remember this principle every time that you are confronted with this kind of event: *Praise in public. Criticise in private.*

The Principle of Forgiveness

Mistakes can hurt your spouse depending on the gravity of what you have done wrong. Forgetting to turn off the faucet might not really cause so much pain, but physically hurting your wife will cause not just physical, but psychological and emotional pain as well. In the same way, you can also be hurt by the mistakes, blunders and errors of your spouse. And what's the natural tendency of individuals when they get hurt? Yes, it's resentment.

More than the skills needed to weather the storm, strength of character is also essential for a person to forgive. As Mahatma Gandhi famously said, *"The weak can never forgive. Forgiveness is the attribute of the strong."* But how can you forgive a person, who is supposed to love and cherish you, but instead hurts you so much? Being hurt by anybody is painful, but being hurt by your spouse is horrible. And most of the time, instead of aiming for reconciliation, couples tend to resent one another, wait for opportunity to make things even, and grow apart during the process.

Resentment does nothing good except to hurt the person who choose to hold on to it. And in the case of married couples, resentment can hurt the relationship as well. A Chinese proverb says, *"Holding on to anger is like grasping a hot coal with the intent of throwing it at someone else; you are the one who gets burned."* When your spouse made a mistake that made you really angry and you decide to hold on to that emotion, then everything will be affected in your relationship. In fact, every other mistake, no matter how small it is, will be magnified by the resentment that you are nurturing in your heart.

The Principle of Forgiveness states that as much as you are willing to go out of your way to correct the mistakes of your spouse, you must also be willing to give your trust once again and forgive your partner unconditionally. It is not easy, I know. But it's the only way for you to truly learn out of the experience and grow as individuals and as a couple. As the Bible says in Ephesians 4:26, *" 'In your anger do not sin': Do not let the sun go down while you are still angry, and do not give the devil a foothold."*

The Principle of Self-Responsibility

James McNulty, a psychologist at the University of Tennessee, conducted a study along with his colleagues to analyse the factors that affect the marital satisfaction of couples. One aspect that they studied is the way that couples handle their conflicts and disagreements as well as mistakes and faults that happen along the way. 251 newly wed couples were the subject of the study and they were contacted at least eight times over the duration of four years.

Included in the research carried out by McNulty is the tendency of couples to blame each other over any negative behaviour or other blunders done by their spouse. Using the data gathered in their study, they noted that those couples who are more satisfied with their marriage adopt a liberal behaviour when it comes to the mistakes of their partners. It means that they see mistakes as something that is outside of their partner's control. On the other hand, those couples who have more problems seem to adopt a blame-game strategy. In short, any mistake or bad act must be the fault of one of them.

McNulty said, *"If your partner on average is rarely engaging in negative behaviors, if you don't have many problems, then it's best to give the partner the benefit of the doubt. Even if your partner deserves to be held accountable for a specific event, if it doesn't happen very often, it's better to sort of look the other way, to look at the bright side."* What McNulty is saying is that we should always assume the best from our partner. Our spouses are not usually out there to get us with the intention of inflicting hurt, thus, if they committed something that is painful, it would be wise to give it the benefit of the doubt and think that it was unintentional.

However, here's the caveat, still according to McNulty. He added, *"If you have a partner who's constantly getting into trouble, having problems outside the relationship, inside the relationship, if they're big problems, then it's not such a good idea to look the other way."* Both of you must have adhered to the *Principle of Self-Responsibility* and be accountable to each other when it comes to mistakes and slipups committed. No one should blame anyone, but instead you must mutually work together to fix whatever mistakes that you find inside the relationship. You are able. You have the capacity. And you are responsible.

Handling mistake and confronting the person who made the error is never easy. It is always a tricky situation. On one hand, you want the person to learn that what he did is wrong by correcting him. But on the other hand, you don't want that correction to be a start of the strain in your relationship. I stand firmly on my belief that correction is essential to growth.

If you have already established a deep sense of trust to each other, then correction might be easier. However, if you are just beginning to practise the discipline, then you don't have to worry. Just live by the *Principles of Correction* and I can guarantee you that you will be able to handle the conflict with grace and love and can even use it as a tool to help you in deepening your intimacy and strengthening your relationship.

Practical Tips to Correct

As I have said earlier, I firmly believe that healthy correction of mistakes in accordance with the right principles is essential to have a more satisfying married life. Since mistakes are bound to happen to imperfect individuals who are in imperfect relationships, then it is crucial to learn the concepts surrounding the right way to correct a person in relation to the mistakes that he made. In this last section of this chapter, let me give you some practical tips and advice that can further increase your knowledge when it comes to correcting.

Keep the In-Laws Out

One of the most heated debates throughout the ages is whether in-laws help or distract the marriage of their sons and daughters. We all know the concept of mentorship and the importance of learning from those people who are ahead of us. But it seems the rules are different when it comes to marriage. Some people say that in-laws must be allowed to interfere because they have the wealth of experience when it comes to marital relationship that they can pass to their children. On the other hand, some people are saying that in-laws must be kept out because they might have different motives in their interference in their children's marriage and might not think based on what's the best for the spouses.

To shed some light into this issue, a research was conducted by Terri Orbuch, a psychologist and research professor at the University of Michigan's Institute for Social Research. Her study subjected 373 newly wed couples in 1986 and followed them for 26 years. The goal of her study is to understand the dynamics of the relationships of those married couples in connection with their closeness to their in-laws. Each of the couples was asked about how close they felt they are to their in-laws and then tracked their relationships over time.

The results of the study were revealing. Orburch found out that when the husband reported having a close relationship with his in-laws, the risk of divorce for the couple was decreased by 20%. But when wives became close to their in-laws, the risk of divorce tend to increase by 20%. The result of the study speaks a lot about the dynamics of couples and in-laws relationship.

According to Orburch, husbands see their in-laws as an extension of his own family – a new mom and dad, if you may. She said, *"Close in-law ties between a husband and his wife's parents are reinforcing to women and connect him to her. When a husband gets close to his wife's parents, this says to her: 'Your family is important to me because I care about you. I want to feel closer to them because it makes me feel closer to you.' And of course, that makes us women feel really good."*

The dynamics are a little different when it comes to women. Wives have the tendency to be closer to her husband's parents when there are some issues with her spouse that's been bothering her and she wants to change it. Or perhaps the couple have differences in opinion when it comes to certain matters such as child-rearing and she would seek the opinions of her in-laws to get them on her side. This idea is not healthy for several reasons. First, the husband will feel that his wife and his parents are ganging up against him. Second, the closeness of the mother of the husband to thedaughter-in-law will mean that there will be greater access to talk and might be an avenue to meddle with some issues in this young family.

Orburch further said, *"If women are close to their in-laws, especially early in their marriage, this interferes with or prevents them from forming a unified and strong bond with their husband. Also, since women are constantly analysing and trying to improve their relationships, they often take what their in-laws say as personal and can't set the clear boundaries."*

As much as you can learn a lot from what your parents have gone through, you must still not let them to meddle with the affairs of your relationship especially when dealing with correction of mistakes. This can result in your parents getting furious with your spouse or vice versa and might force them to interfere in your marital relationship because they might get the idea that you still don't know what you are doing.

Focus on One Topic at a Time

Try to imagine this scenario. You are sitting on the couch watching your favourite show on TV when suddenly your wife lashed at you, *"Hey Mister. Aren't you being too comfortable just sitting there, acting high and mighty, while watching the TV? Can't you see that there are a lot of things that need to be done in the kitchen?"* You were startled at first, but you realise she's right. So you stand up and as you walk over to the kitchen to do the dish, she yells again at you, *"Hey Mister! Aren't you being too comfortable walking over to the kitchen, acting high and mighty, without turning off that TV?!"* You want to shoot back, but you just go over to the TV and turn it off. As you head over to the kitchen, for the third time your wife howled at you, *"Hey Mister! Can you walk faster and do the dishes immediately? After that you must fix your things in the drawer. I don't want being surrounded by mess!"*

How do you think will you respond to the demands of your wife? Probably you will get mad at her and shout, *"Hey Miss! Can't you see I'm only one person! Let me deal with it one thing at a time!"* Dealing with mistakes and correction must also be done in the same way. Focus on one thing at a time. Don't bring in past grievances, worries, and other things that might clutter the issue at hand. If you want to confront your husband because of how he acted in front of your friends last night, then talk only about that topic. Don't try to bring up the things that he did last month or the fact that he didn't fix the bed earlier in the morning. Let the discussion focus on one single topic. If you still want to resolve the other matters of concern, then solve it in succession and not simultaneously.

Allow Your Spouse to Respond

If there is one thing that will truly damage your effort in confronting the mistakes, then it's not giving enough time for your spouse to respond. Someone once said that we judge ourselves by our intentions but we judge other people by their actions. It means that when we do something questionable, we justify it by saying that we just want what is best for the relationship. However, when our spouse is the one who did something wrong, we immediately dismiss the presumption that she is innocent and assume that he intentionally did it to hurt you.

Allowing your spouse to respond will help both of you to clarify the issue. If you are having some presumption about the mistake that was committed, hearing the side of your spouse will shed some light and will confirm whether what you have in mind is true or you are just allowing your imagination to run wild. In Chapter 4, I mentioned the concept of *Conference Conversation* where both of you will give time to listen to each other as you explain each other's side. This tip carries the same idea.

Learn to listen to what your spouse has to say. Remember, the goal in any conflict resolution is not for someone to apologise. The goal of conflict resolution and confrontation about mistakes is to have clarity about the matter and pave the way for the restoration of your relationship. Author Bryant McGill once said, *"One of the most sincere forms of respect is actually listening to what the other person has to say."*

Balance Correction with Love

As you already know, correcting your spouse increases the possibility that you might hurt him or her. That is to be expected.

Having another person come up to us and tell us that we are wrong can hurt our pride and ego; hence the dilemma of correction. But there is one way to address this dilemma that will help you to make the process more bearable and at the same time improve the relationship. It's balancing correction with love.

I mentioned before that according to studies, the ideal ratio of negative to positive feedbacks between spouses must be one is to five. It means that in every negative comment, it must be balanced with five expressions of love. The same ratio can be applied when you are going to correct your spouse over a mistake that he made. You can express your disappointments and your frustrations about his or her actions but don't let it stop there. Express your love in various ways. Balance your correction with lots of affection and you can benefit greatly from the growth of your spouse while at the same time strengthen your marriage.

Correction is Essential

Mistakes and imperfections are inevitable in marriage. But that is only one side of the coin. The other side is something that most people do not see in the context of marital union, and that is correction. It can also be painful. If not handled properly, it may also strain the relationship that you have with your spouse. However, it is essential for growth. As much as corrections from the teacher are important to see areas that require improvement in different subjects in school, correction from your spouse is also equally important to see areas of growth that you can still exploit.

Let me end this story by recounting one of the most famous stories in the Bible that speaks about the pain of sin, and the sting of correction. It's the account of David's adultery with Bathsheba and his murder of Bathsheba's husband – Uriah. Everything that David had done displeased God. And though he was already the mighty king of Israel, David was rebuked by a prophet. Prophet Nathan said in 2 Samuel 12:9, *"Why have you despised the word of the LORD by doing evil in His sight? You have struck down Uriah the Hittite with the sword, have taken his wife to be your wife, and have killed him with the sword of the sons of Ammon."*

It probably hurt David. The sting of correction is real. But instead of resisting Nathan and defending his position, David humbly said in verse 13, *"I have sinned against the Lord."* Because of correction, David realised his folly and immediately repented of the things that he did. Correction has been essential to his life. In the same way, correction is essential for both you and your spouse. Yes, it might sting, but the reflections and realisations that you will gain will be priceless gems of truth that will help you to improve your relationship.

Reflection Questions:

This portion of each chapter aims to help you and your spouse to properly evaluate the principles and concepts that you have learned. Try to answer all the questions truthfully. Discuss it with your spouse so you can gain a greater insight when it comes to your partner's ideas and personal thoughts. It will also be helpful if you could share your answers with another couple who might be delighted to go in the journey with you.

1. Before reading this chapter, how did you view correction? Did you use to hate it and avoid it at all costs? Do you believe that it is essential to improve the relationship of married couples? Reflect on the four ways of dealing with mistakes, namely, the *Nice Guy,* the *Beast,* the *Martyr,* and the *Righteous Judge,* where do you usually stand? What do you think are the underlying reasons why you respond to correction in that particular manner?

_____

_____

_____

2. What are your principles when it comes to dealing with mistakes? Identify a specific time where you needed to confront your spouse about a specific blunder that he made. How did you respond to that incident? Did you intentionally talk to other people about it and in essence brought the matter to the open or did you protect your spouse's privacy and talked to him about it in private? On a scale of 1 to 5, 1 being the lowest and 5 the highest, how confident can you say that you handle corrections in the spirit of love, respect and dignity. Elaborate on your answers.

_____

_____

3. Do you have the tendency to blame your spouse about anything bad that happens in your relationship? Do you automatically presume about the wrong motives of your spouse and his intention in doing wrong instead of giving him the benefit of the doubt? Explain. How much forgiveness are you willing to give to your offending spouse? If you believe in the Bible, then do you take Jesus at His Word saying that we must forgive other people seventy times seven?

_____

_____

_____

4. What is your perspective about the interference of in-laws in a couple's relationship? How do you handle the situation with in-laws in your own marriage? In relation to the issue of correction, do you normally discuss the matter by focusing on one topic at a time? On what ways can you balance correction with love? Think of different ideas of what you can do in your marriage to make sure that you balance the negative with lots of expression of love.

_____

_____

_____

SIXTH CRITERION: MAXIMIZING CONNECTION IN MARRIAGE

CHAPTER 8

"It is not a lack of love, but a lack of friendship that makes unhappy marriages."

– Friedrich Nietzsche

Some people believe that couples who are already married are those people who have found the person that they strongly connected with. That's why most of us are fascinated and enthralled when we see a close friend or a relative that is tying the knot. We normally say, *"It's good for him…"* or *"She's so lucky!"* However, if those assumptions are true, then why does divorce still exist? Does that mean that the concept of connection within the bounds of marital union is not really that strong?

In the observation of Diane Coutu, the Director of client communications at Banyan Family Business Advisors, she noticed that most of the extra-marital affairs that is causing divorce between married couples did not really stem from sexual attraction. It's something else. It's a problem of connection. Coutu said, *"Most affairs are not about sex at all; they're friendship. They're about finding somebody who finds you interesting, attractive, and fascinating."*

Deep friendship within marriage is a function of connection. Without friendship, the relationship between spouses is bound to crumble or to die. In this chapter, we will explore the concept of connection. We will discuss the different categories of connections that happen between spouses. Then, we will elaborate on the importance of connection to create a lasting marriage and lastly, I will give you some practical tips that you can use to improve connection within your marriage.

Different Categories of Connection

Married couples are connected in a lot of ways. And the strength of these connections will dictate whether the marriage will continue to provide satisfaction to husband and wife, or whether their relationship will be a source of grief and sorrow for them and for their whole family.

Before we proceed, let us first have a thorough understanding of the definition and concept of connection. We normally hear the word connection when we talk about our mobile devices. When you have a wi-fi connection, or you are connected to a wi-fi network, then you can utilise that connection to browse the internet, download music, or even watch a movie. In short, when you are connected, you can take advantage of the benefits that are being provided by that particular wi-fi access.

On the other hand, when your mobile phone has no signal, it means that it is not connected to your network provider. Without that connection, then you can't send messages, make a call, or browse the social media. Though, mobile devices are flawed analogy, it carries the same idea when it comes to connection in marriage. Marital connection is a bond. It is a link that must not be broken but be protected at all times. If your connection to your spouse is strong, then both of you can experience the happiness and satisfaction that marriage can provide. In other words, both of you can enjoy the benefits of being married.

We will talk more about the specific benefits of connection, but for now, here are the different connections that you must guard when it comes to your marital relationship.

Connection by Covenant

When both of you faced each other in front of the altar, utter the wedding oaths that you prepared for one another, and placed the wedding ring in each other's finger, then you have been bound by the connection that is given by having a covenant. This is the most basic and the most tangible form of connection that married couples have.

However, though the agreement might be written by ink on a piece of paper, the covenant that each of you made must remain deeply within each other's heart. That covenant must be protected till the end and must not be exposed to unnecessary risks and dangers such as the temptation to become unfaithful.

Connection by Emotion

Spouses are also connected through the emotions and feelings that they have for each other. The love, the affection, and the intimacy that they share together are the foundation of their emotional connection. It is intangible but can be visibly seen by people around the couple. A simple glance, sharing short and sweet conversations, and even the holding of hands show evidences of the connection that the couples have.

You must understand that emotional connection does not grow on its own. It is entirely dependent on the things that you say or do for your spouse. Being thoughtful, showing acts of kindness and being liberal with affirmation all contribute in strengthening this kind of connection.

Connection by Flesh

Our modern world and culture might have differing views about the issue of sex, but in the Bible it is clearly stated that physical intimacy through sexual intercourse is reserved only for the marriage bed. The Bible says in Hebrews 13:4, *"Marriage should be honoured by all, and the marriage bed kept pure, for God will judge the adulterer and the sexually immoral."* It means that sex is meant to be shared only between married spouses.

Now, you might believe that that thinking is a little bit old-fashioned, but that principle is what I firmly believe in. The connection in the flesh must only be shared with one person and one person only, and that is your spouse.

Well, is there any benefit in waiting other than you are honouring God by obeying His words? Surprisingly, there is. A study was conducted by colleagues from the University of Virginia called *"Before I Do."* It is focused on the fundamental effects and consequences of what a couple do before they tie the knot, in relation to their marital satisfaction and overall happiness in the relationship.

The psychologists Galena Rhoades and Scott Stanley, who contributed in the 2014 study said that couples who wait for marriage before they participate in sexual intercourse are among the happiest couples. They said, *"In general, couples who wait to have sex later in their relationship report higher levels of marital quality."*

Considering these aspects of connections in marriage, it is therefore essential for any married couples to invest the time, effort, and energy needed in cultivating these connections in their everyday lives. No married spouses must leave connection to do its own job, instead they must work together at it, making sure that the covenant is protected, their emotional connections are being deepened, and the physical connections are being properly utilised and enjoyed.

Connection and its Role in Building Lasting Marriages

If there is one thing that will have considerable impact in marital satisfaction and also serves as a useful gauge in predicting the longevity of marriage, then it is the criterion of connection. Think about it, in every aspect of our lives, connection is everything. If your mobile device is not connected to a network service provider, then it is basically useless. In the same way, if your electronic appliances are not connected to an electrical outlet, then it is also of no use. If you are not connected to the outside world, then you will miss a lot of opportunities that might help you to advance in your life. Here are some principles that highlight the role of connection in building lasting marriages.

Connection Influences Everything

Let's say for example that you have everything that you want. You have an awesome house that is built with high-quality materials including the latest electronic devices and appliances that you can find in the market. You have several cars in your garage and a multi-million business that can provide everything that you need materially. In addition to these possessions, you also have three adorable children who perfectly love and care for one another. What more can you ask for?

However, your connection with your spouse has recently hit the rock. You are not talking like you used to and have totally alienated yourselves each other. Tell me, will you still experience the bliss in your marriage? Assuming that you don't want to cut off the relationship, can you maximise the enjoyment with all the possessions that you have, knowing that you share these things with a person that you don't really have a connection with? Indeed, connection influences everything.

Connection Deepens the Relationship

Every couple who genuinely loves each other started with building connections. They tried to find things that they value together, they talk about things that they have shared interests in and they tried to find common ground just to connect with each other. If they have differing opinions, they talk about it, share their views, and try to understand each other all in the name of connection. And along the process of connecting, their relationship also deepens.

It doesn't only work for new couples who are in the early stage of their romantic relationships. In fact, I would go as far to say that connection has power over the entire duration of their relationship. Neglect it and the bond will be stalled. Work on it and the relationship will just get deeper.

However, you must understand that a lot of couples choose to neglect it because connecting with another person is a difficult thing to do. It is much easier to always have your way in things, not thinking about the things that matter to the other person. But if you will choose the path of connection, then I can guarantee that as much as your relationship gets deeper in its early stages, it can also enhance your relationship in its current state. Connection never loses its power.

This is How to Connect

I believe that every individual has the knowledge to connect. The level of understanding of the basic concepts of connection might differ, but we all know how to connect nonetheless. Connecting with another person is specially highlighted when it comes to romantic relationships. Couples take the effort needed just to know one another and at the same develop the kind of connection that will sustain a loving relationship.

However, it is also common for romantic couples to fall out of love or more accurately, to fall in love with another person to whom they can establish a more stable and a more thrilling connection. Thus, it is crucial for married couples who seriously intend to stay together to learn and re-learn the fundamental principles of connecting with each other. Here are some practical pieces of advice that you can try in improving the bond in your relationship.

Spend Time Together

It goes without saying that the best way to connect with your spouse involves physical presence. It's hard to connect with someone who might be miles away from you. Though, it is not impossible, but why would you like to experience it if your spouse is just a few feet away from you? Spending time together means taking enough amount of time to talk, bond, or even just stare at each other and wonder how you ended up with this person, and then share a good laugh!

Spending quality time with your other half is one of the basic ways to connect. You don't have to go to an expensive restaurant or travel to another country together. You can spend your time together while eating at the kitchen table and sharing your experiences all throughout the day. You can just sit on the porch, read to each other, or just simply appreciate the beautiful sunset together. I will encourage you to be creative in this aspect. Find time to do a common interest and don't be afraid to try to do new things in your relationship.

Just an advice: When talking about spending time, it is of utmost importance that you write down on your schedule the specific hours and dates that you are to devote with one another. Remember, next week is not a date so make sure that you are specific with the schedule. For instance, if you know that there is an upcoming holiday, then you can already arrange everything even months before.

Be Each Other's Best Friend

If I will you ask a series of questions about your spouse right now, can you answer it right away without any hint of hesitation? Let's try. Try to answer these questions in the presence of your spouse and see how many correct answers you will get.

1. What is the favourite colour of your spouse?
2. What is the current struggle of your partner that he or she is having a hard time dealing with?
3. What is your spouse's favourite place to eat dinner other than your house?
4. Who is the favourite movie actor or actress of your spouse and why?
5. When can you say that your spouse is irritated or stressed?

Did you get all the answers correctly? As you can see, these are some of the basic questions that we normally share with our best friends. Sadly, most couples have a hard time telling their spouse the things that they want to talk about, but do not find any problem sharing the same things to their best friend? But what if you try the other path? Treat your spouse as your best of friends, and tell him or her all the things that are going on in your mind. Give your partner your best in everything that you do. As Dave Willis said, "*Always strive to give your spouse the very best of yourself; not what's left over after you have given your best to everyone else."*

In a research conducted by the National Bureau of Economic Research in Canada, the researchers were able to find out and confirm that married people are happier compared to being single. The study used the combined data of the British Household Panel Survey, the United Kingdom's Annual Population Survey and the Gallup World Poll to come up with this conclusion. One of the primary ways that happiness is bolstered in marriage is when couples consider each other as their "best friends." In addition to this, the wellbeing benefits that this kind of couples receive are the highest.

Give Each Other Massages

Well, this one for me is just outright creative. If you are like most couples, then you probably haven't tried yet giving massages to each other. However, studies show that there are tremendous benefits when couples participate in spending a couple of hours just rubbing down each other's body in a non-sensual way.

Esther Boykin, a licensed marriage and family therapist and also a co-founder of Group Therapy Associates, shares the sentiment of the power of connection between couples who massage each other. She said, *"During a massage session, people are almost instinctually driven to let go of the past and the future and turn their attention to the present moment. This practice of being fully engaged in an activity together that can help couples reconnect, and with little effort, they can bring that same level of mindful awareness to their time outside of the massage."*

If you don't have practical knowledge about massage, then you can always watch a video online, read a book or just get some sessions on organisations and groups that teach massage therapy. Stef Safran, a dating expert, quipped regarding the benefits of massage, *"A couple's massage is pretty much a scientific love potion."*

Connection Is Indispensable

Connection between you and your spouse can help in determining the marital satisfaction and bliss as well as the longevity of your marriage. Admittedly, connection is a difficult thing to achieve, but the rewards of a strong and deep bond with your spouse will always be worth the effort. If you are ready to take your marriage to the next level, then you can't neglect connecting with your spouse. I challenge you to become creative. Find what works and what doesn't work for your relationship. Don't be afraid to try new things. Just remember, in marriage, connection is absolutely indispensable.

Reflection Questions:

This portion of each chapter aims to help you and your spouse to properly evaluate the principles and concepts that you have learned. Try to answer all the questions truthfully. Discuss it with your spouse so you can gain a greater insight when it comes to your partner's ideas and personal thoughts. It will also be helpful if you could share your answers with another couple who might be delighted to go in the journey with you.

1. On a scale of 1 to 10, where 1 is the lowest and 10 is the highest, rate the level of connection that you have with your spouse? Based on your assessment, are you satisfied with the level of connection that you have when it comes to your marriage as a whole? How about the level of emotional connection that you have? The physical connection?

2. Do you believe in the notion that all people – especially couples – have a basic understanding of the concepts of connection and the benefits that it brings? Why or why not? Do you agree that connection can help in determining whether the marriage will last and be full of happiness or just remain stagnant and eventually crumble? Elaborate on your answers.

3. What are the different ways that you both used as a couple to connect with one another during the early years of your relationship? Are you still utilising those methods? If yes, then do you still find it an effective tool to boost your connection? If no, then what methods are you currently using to deepen the

connection between you and your spouse?

_____

_____

_____

4. What other ways can you think that could help you and your
    spouse to build a stronger connection? Get a calculator, and
    compute the percentage of time that you usually give to your
    spouse in a week. For instance, we have 7 days a week, which
    constitute 168 hours a week. If you are spending roughly an
    hour a day with your spouse, meaning you are give your
    partner 90% to 100% of your focus attention for 7 hours a
    week, it is equivalent to 4% of your week's life. (*7H divide by
    168H*) Are you happy with the answer that you get? If not, then
    immediately think of ways that you can increase this rate, at all
    costs.

_____

_____

_____

SEVENTH CRITERION: MAKING THE MOST OF CONSUMMATION

CHAPTER 9

"Sex is God's gift to express intimacy at a level that words cannot comprehend."

– Chip Ingram

In a survey conducted by National Opinion Research Centre, they found out that an average American couple participate in sexual intercourse 66 times a year. However, in another study conducted by Newsweek, there is also a growing number of couples, around 15% to 20%, who are having sex only for an average of 10 times a year. This is considered as a *"sexless marriage."* The results of the study raise a considerable concern about the importance of sex in any marital relationship.

Try to create your own assessment. How many times did you and your spouse make love last week? How about last month or the last quarter? Is the number of times that you have sex increasing or significantly decreasing? Does the frequency of sexual intercourse affect your marriage in a positive or a negative way? These are questions that only the two of you can answer.

I firmly believe that one of the greatest gifts of God to mankind is the ability to enjoy and take pleasure from sexual activities. At the same time, I also believe that this kind of activity should only be offered to and received from your spouse. Considering these ideas, it will be obvious that I'm a big believer that every couple must do their best to make the best out of their sexual intimacy –

the consummation of their marriage.

"Ideal love making in marriage is born out of a deep passion for each other mingled with strong desire for bonding and pleasure" Chindah Chindah

Still, it is also common knowledge to most married couples that there is a variety of problems that might hamper couples to take pleasure in this exclusive and intimate activity. This chapter will focus on the importance of sexual intimacy in marriage. The common problems with regards to sex of married couples will also be discussed and lastly, some principles to have great sex will be elaborated.

The Importance of Sexual Intimacy

Though I don't believe and advocate pre-marital sex, I'm a staunch supporter and encourager when it comes to sexual intimacy inside the boundaries of marriage. I believe that couples who already tied the knot must experience the greatest satisfaction of becoming one in the flesh with their spouses. One reason for this is because I know and understand the tremendous importance and benefits of sex for married couples. Here are some of the most notable advantages of sexual intimacy that you can think about.

Sex Deepens the Bond and Knowledge

The first mention of the idea of sex in the Bible is located in the book of Genesis, specifically in Chapter 4, verse 1. The Bible says, *"And Adam knew Eve his wife; and she conceived, and bare Cain, and said, I have gotten a man from the LORD." (Genesis 4:1 KJV)* This verse speaks of the sexual intercourse of Adam and Eve and the subsequent pregnancy and delivery by Eve of Cain.

The thing that is truly fascinating is the choice of words that the Bible used. *"Adam knew Eve."* The Bible used the Hebrew word *"Ya-dah"*, which literally means *"to know"* to denote sex. This idea speaks of the importance of sexual intimacy in deepening the knowledge of spouses about each other. When couples make love to each other, they are genuinely becoming vulnerable to each other. They are allowing their mates to know the most intimate part of their body while at the same time gaining knowledge about the urges and desires of their partners.

That is why the Bible says regarding marriage that couples who marry become one person. It means that they will gain a near-perfect knowledge about each other in their relationship and one way to do that is through sexual intimacy.

Sex Brings Various Medical Benefits

Time and time again, scientists and researchers are concluding that having sex with your spouse brings a lot of benefits to your physical, mental and emotional health. From reducing stress while at the same time increasing the satisfaction that you receive in marriage, sexual intimacy with your spouse is guaranteed to give you the ability to experience not just pleasure, but also the health benefits that it brings. Below are some of the amazing benefits of sex in marriage. (*Source:* TheSpruce.com)

Emotional Benefits of Having Sex:

- Boosts levels of commitment
- Improves self-esteem
- Makes a person feel younger
- Lowers the level of cortisol, a hormone that can trigger fatigue and cravings
- Decreases feelings of insecurity
- Keeps spouses connected emotionally
- Helps to give people a more positive attitude
- Makes a person calmer
- Makes a person less irritable
- Reduces sense of depression
- Relieves stress

Physical Benefits of Having Sex

WHAT CAN I DO TO MAKE MY MARRIAGE WORK?

- Decreases the risk of physical illness
- Boosts immunity
- Reduces pain by increasing endorphins
- Sex is a form of exercise *(200 calories are burnt up every 30 minutes of active sex)*
- Decreases chance of contacting colds and flu
- Lubricates vaginal tissue
- Lower mortality rates
- Reduce risk of prostate cancer for men
- Offers pain relief, including pain from migraines and back pain
- Improves posture
- Provides a youthful glow
- Lessen risk of heart disease
- Helps prevent yeast infections
- Alleviates menstrual periods and cramps
- Firms stomach and buttocks
- Lowers blood pressure
- Helps people sleep better
- Improves digestion
- Improves sense of smell
- Sex provides a therapeutic effect on immune system
- Better bladder control
- Healthier teeth
- Increase DHEA which makes your skin healthier
- Improves fitness level
- Increases circulation
- Improves memory
- Produces chemical in the brain to stimulate growth of new dendrites
- Improves pelvic muscle tone

- Boosts libido

Indeed, just looking at this long list of benefits can encourage you to consistently have sex with your spouse. Dr. Pamela Rogers, MS, PhD said in an informative article about the benefits of sex, *"Sexual experience and satisfaction are closely correlated with overall quality of life. They increase your sense of well-being and personal satisfaction. Sexual activity is negatively correlated with the risk and incidence of psychiatric illness, depression, and suicide. Sexual activity and orgasm reduce stress. Sexual satisfaction is also associated with the stability of relationships."*

Sex Creates a Unique Connection

Sharing sexual intimacy with one person and one person only can create a unique connection between the two of you. Think about this. If your spouse is the only person who you have given your body, and he shares the same sentiment with you, then it means that you have a unique connection that transcends the intimacy of a friend or a relative. Sexual intimacy becomes the single-most important factor that separates your relationship from other platonic friendships and even blood relations.

When people engage in sexual activity, they are giving total access to any parts of their body to their partners. No one but your partner can gain this connection with you, thus it strengthens your security with regards to the relationship. In addition, the benefits that were mentioned above can only be maximized when you have a single person that you consider your trusted sex partner, which should be your spouse.

Common Problems in Sexual Intimacy

No matter how great the benefits that sex can provide to married couples, problems and issues can still creep in if both of them are not willing to guard the intimacy that they have. Sometimes, the human nature of selfishness might get in the way. Advancing age, stress and pressure at work, challenges of raising children, and even familiarity can be the root cause of these problems. Ignoring these issues might not be healthy, not just in sexual intimacy, but for the relationship as a whole. Therefore, couples must immediately address them.

Laziness in bed

Sex provides great pleasure, but at the same time, it also requires spouses to go out of their way and provide that pleasure to each other. Let's face it: There are times when we don't just want to do it. It takes a lot of effort and strength on your part particularly if you are the aggressor in bed. Laziness to do your part to stimulate your partner might leave you both frustrated and hurt.

Boredom to have sex

There might come a time when you and your spouse might think that you have tried it all. You have done all the positions, spoken every word to arouse each other and just resign to the thought that having sex with your partner is just a bore. This is a dangerous situation especially if your spouse's love language is physical touch. Your lack of initiative and creativity might leave your partner wondering whether you still love her.

Exploitation

The possibility of being exploited is also a problem even in marital relationships. Having sex just for the sake of satisfying your urges, then leaving your partner after you had it can create a deep wound in your relationship. The theory that men do it for pleasure, while women do it for love is still in effect even if you have been married for years. And getting sexual satisfaction without satisfying the emotional needs of your spouse is just outright exploitation.

Differing Level of Sexual Drives

Sometimes, your drive and urge to get in bed with your spouse might not match the intensity of her drive to do the same. This is common and without any evidence to the contrary, must not affect the security that you feel regarding the love that you have for each other. However, if not properly handled, this might cause a much deeper issue such as lack of trust and even infidelity.

Principles of Great Sex in Marriage

If you sincerely desire to spice up your marriage or bring it to another level of intimacy, then you can't ignore the need to learn the principles of having a great sex in your relationship. Though I won't provide you with detailed step-by-step plan on how you can please one another in bed, I will lead you to think about the principles of what makes having sex with your spouse one of the best experiences that you can have in your marriage.

Sexual Intimacy is a Gift

As I have said in the beginning of this chapter, I firmly believe that sex should only be enjoyed exclusively by married couples. If you also believe in this notion, then you won't be having a hard time seeing sex as a priceless gift from God. It is a unique connection that only you and your spouse can enjoy. And indeed, receiving pleasure from the person that you genuinely love by his or her touch and giving extreme happiness through the passion that you exert in sex is one of the most important gifts that you can give to each other.

When you see sexual intimacy as a gift your mentality will shift from, *"Just do it"* to *"I must enjoy it fully"*. And if it is a gift, then you should return the favour by showing your love in other aspects of your marriage.

Frequency Matters

A question that usually pop up when talking about sex in marriage is how frequent should it be. Though, there is no magic number that will tell us the exact number of times that you should be intimate in bed, there are different studies and researches conducted to determine how many times do happiest couples have sex.

Based on a research published by Society for Personality and Social Psychology, couples who have sex once a week are considered the happiest. The result is based on a 40-year study of 30,000 Americans who were surveyed. However, Amy Muise, the lead researcher says, *"Although more frequent sex is associated with greater happiness, this link was no longer significant at a frequency of more than once a week. Our findings suggest that it's important to maintain an intimate connection with your partner, but you don't need to have sex everyday as long as you're maintaining that connection."*

Yes, frequency matters, but it's more important to be intimately connected with your spouse whether you are having sex or not.

Sex is for both of you

Sex must always be for the pleasure of both spouses. If only one of the couple is always enjoying the experience, then there must be something wrong. More than the pleasure that each of the spouses feels, they must also be considerate enough to give chance to their spouse to explain some ideas where they can experience more pleasure. In other words, sexual activities must be planned and discussed. You don't have to just jump on the bed and start doing your thing. No, you must be able to listen to each other to ensure that both of you will experience the highest intensity of pleasure from your sexual intimacy.

Make the Most of it!

If you are not currently enjoying your sexual life with your spouse, then something must be done. Remember that sex is one of the single-most important connections that you and your partner have. No one can share that connection with you. And no one must share the sexual intimacy with your partner too. Considering these facts, then you must make it a priority to make the most out of it. Visit places, read books about it, and don't be afraid that your spouse might look differently at you. If there's one thing that must not be removed from sexual intimacy between married couples, it is the freedom to decide which activity will suit them best.

Do it. Enjoy it. Have great sex. And do it more frequently.

Reflection Questions:

This portion of each chapter aims to help you and your spouse to properly evaluate the principles and concepts that you have learned. Try to answer all the questions truthfully. Discuss it with your spouse so you can gain a greater insight when it comes to your partner's ideas and personal thoughts. It will also be helpful if you could share your answers with another couple who might be delighted to go in the journey with you.

1. In your own perception, rate the importance of sexual intimacy in your marriage. Based on your answer, kindly elaborate whether you see sexual intimacy as one of the fundamental aspects of your relationship. Do you do it with sufficient regularity and intentionality or you don't really care whether you do it or not?

_____

_____

_____

2. What benefits and advantages have you reaped from having sex with your partner? Do you believe that having sex regularly can make your marriage happier and lasting? What actions will you take to make sure that you will make the most of this gift of sexual intimacy?

_____

_____

3. What are the common problems that you encounter in the aspect of sexual intimacy? What do you think are the causes of these problems? What particular steps will you take to address these issues and make sure that it won't hinder you in enjoying sexual intimacy with your spouse?

_____

_____

4. When was the last time you had sex with your partner? What are the circumstances surrounding it? Did you schedule and plan it or did it happen based on impulse? In your sexual activities, what is your primary motive? Do you consider whether you please your spouse or do you usually put your own pleasure ahead of your partner's happiness?

_____

_____

_____

EIGHTH CRITERION: EMPLOYING IDEAS OF CONSERVATION

CHAPTER 10

"Marriage is about love. Divorce is about money."

– Anonymous

There are a lot of things that can cause pressure and stress in marriages across the globe. But in a recent survey conducted by SunTrust Bank, the researchers found out that the leading cause of stress in a relationship is finance. 35% of people who were surveyed said that money was the primary cause of friction in their relationship.

In addition to financial stress in relationships, it also seems that a growing number of couples are having trust issues when it comes to money. In a poll conducted by CreditCards.com, the results showed that one in every five Americans have spent $500 or more and kept it hidden to their partners. And though a few minority, there are 6% of those who answered the poll who admitted that they are holding secret bank accounts and credit cards from their partners.

If you have been married for quite some time, then I believe that you can relate to the fact of how stressing the area of finance is for married couples. It doesn't matter whether you are earning much or earning low compared to an average couple. Money problems seem to exist across marriages and thus the need to address it wisely. In this chapter, we will talk about the matter of money inside a marital relationship. We will elaborate on the importance and benefits of learning good money management in marriage.

After that, we will discuss the fundamental principles of good money management. And lastly, I will share with you some practical tips that you need to do immediately to manage your finances properly.

Benefits of Good Money Management

I don't know what your view is when it comes to money, but I tell you how important your perception is when it comes to managing your finances. I firmly believe that stress and problems arise in marital finances when spouses have differing views about money.

Here is one common perception that is utterly false: *Money is the root of all evil.* Thinking about how money affects all aspects of life, it seems correct that money can be the root of all evil. However, looking closely at what the Bible really says in 1 Timothy 6:10, *"For the love of money is the root of all kinds of evil."* Now, we're talking. Let's face it. When you love money more than you love your spouse or your family, then problems with finances will inevitably happen. But if you are able to properly handle your finances and have a healthy outlook about money, then you can reap some benefits from it.

Money gives you more options

Surely, money can't buy you happiness, but it can give you a lot of options. When you don't have money, then your options about where you will live, what appliances you will buy, and what gifts you will give to each other will only be limited. You might sincerely love your wife and desire to give her a vacation in the beautiful islands of Hawaii, but if you don't have the money, then vacation in Hawaii can't be on your options.

As a side note, I also believe that no matter how much you earn from your job or your business, if you don't have good money management skills, then you are still bound to be limited when it comes to your options. If you want more choices and a large space for financial decision making, then good money management is a must for both of you.

Less stress in the relationship

As mentioned at the introduction of this chapter, money problems rank as one of the top problems and issues that cause stress for married couples. So if you are able to properly manage inflow and control your outflow, then the stress and pressure caused by finances can be lessened.

I believe that married couples must agree when it comes to financial decisions involving saving, investing and disbursing funds. With a strong system in place and a mutual agreement to honor that system, couples can lessen the stress in the relationship. The system serves as the standard to which both of them must comply.

More time to focus on things that matter more

How many hours do you spend arguing whether you must purchase a new Television set? How many days have you spent arguing about the decision that one of you made without consulting the other? These arguments and quarrels about finances can be eliminated when a good money management system is in place.

You don't have to be experts to do this. There are a plethora of books out there teaching money management principles that are filled with tips and insights that you could use to become a better manager of your finances. All you need is a willing heart to learn, and humility to respect each other's decision when it comes to your finances.

Principles of Good Money Management

Most of the time, what's missing is not the skills needed by couples to manage their finances well. They might know how to produce money, have some knowledge and insights when it comes to budgeting, and also know-hows on different investment vehicles where they can grow their funds and earn some returns. However, what is missing is not those techniques, but the principles underlying those money management techniques.

And when it comes to principles of money management, I

believe that one of the greatest sources of sound and timeless principles to manage your finances is through the Bible. Entrepreneur and motivational speaker, Jim Rohn, once said that when you have money problems, you go to the Bible and there you will learn the things that you might be doing wrong. Here are some biblical principles that you might consider in handling your finances. Even though you are not a person of faith, I believe that what the Bible teaches about money is universal and can be applied to all.

Live beneath your means

Hebrews 13:5 says, *"Don't love money; be satisfied with what you have."* Again, the Bible is warning us that we should not love money. We should not let our hearts set on material wealth and possession and to be satisfied and contented with what we have.

Think about this. There are people who get short in finances whether they make lesser or more money. In other words, their way of living matches the income that they are making. It's like money goes in, then money goes out without any excess for investment or saving. Worse still, some people even spend money outside the money they earn. Couples who are not satisfied with what they have will do everything that they can just to make that purchase even if they have to do it on credit. And before they know it, their debts are way bigger than they can handle. Dave Ramsey say it better. He said, *"We buy things we don't need with money we don't have to impress people we don't like."*

Living beneath your means is the antithesis of this practice. If you are content and satisfied with what you have, then you don't have to purchase luxurious things out of debt. You seriously consider the money that you are making and ensure that your way of living is according to the resources that you hold.

Money is just a tool

One of the most common misconceptions that people have is that money is the way to become truly happy. How many times have we heard the phrase, *"Well, I believe that money can't buy happiness"* and then spend the next 50 hours of the week working just to make a *'little more.'* Other people who have extreme and antagonistic beliefs about money say that the more money you have, the more evil you will become. However, is it true? If you look closely at the characters in the Bible, then you can clearly conclude that they are richly blessed by God in terms of finances.

Couples need to learn that having more money will not automatically make them happier with the companionship of each other. That will be determined by the way they use it. The Bible says in Luke 16:9, *"I tell you, use worldly wealth to gain friends for yourselves..."* You might be making six-digits income per month, but without the capacity to spend it on things that really matter for your well-being, then it won't still make you more satisfied in the relationship.

"Marriages works well when money is mutually handled well"
Chindah Chindah

Motive matters in money management

The motive of why you want to manage your money is one of the crucial aspects that you need to take care of. The Bible says in Proverbs 16:2, *"All a person's ways seem pure to them, but motives are weighed by the LORD."* Why do you want to stop spending money on those *'unnecessary things'?* Is it because you want to save enough money for your children's future? Or you just want to have enough money to purchase that boat? If your heart is not right in money management, then you are bound to fail. If your reason is not strong enough to keep your hand from spending just a little more, then you will just find yourself still squabbling about your finances.

But what is the right motive when it comes to handling your finances? There could be a lot of reasons, but I believe that the best reason is that reason that puts your marriage and your family on top. Remember, money is just a tool. It is neutral. The thing that will determine whether it will work for your benefit or will bite you is the motive inside your heart.

Practical Tips and Insights to Manage your Money

There are a myriad of tips and insights that you can find on the web about handling your finances. Some might sound absurd at first, but there are things that are downright practical and should be done immediately. The things that you will learn here are the basics, but I firmly believe that it will help you have a jumpstart towards managing your finances in a way that you will grow together as a couple.

Sit and talk about the issue

It is settled that one of the most common causes of marital conflicts is money – whether the lack or the abundance of it, the difference in perception, and the ways that couples spend it. You might be a usual saver and believe in the importance of saving up for the future, while your spouse might be a spender and uses the money to experience the best of life as of the moment. As you can see, the difference in their outlook in life might result in friction in the relationship.

The best way to deal with this issue is to sit down and talk about the different issues swirling on the finance aspect of your marriage. Talk freely about your feelings and make sure that each side express their mind. The *Conversation Communication* will be a great way to talk about these issues. Voice out your fears and your frustrations about the way your spouse is handling finances and also listen to his take on the matter. Avoid attacking your partner whilst you insist on talking about the benefits that your family will gain if you will find out how good money management really works.

Decide on a budget and stick to it

Yes, budget is still the most practical tool that you can use when it comes to money management. You might have some knowledge about doing this one so it's time to flex those financial skills and create a budget for your family. Here's a step by step procedure that you can follow:

1. *Use a formula to identify spendable amount.*

   The idea of using a formula is fairly simple. You just have to determine the exact percentages that will be set aside for savings, investment, and spending. A formula might look like this:

   Expenses = Income – Savings (20%) – Tithes/charity (10%)

   For instance, if you make $100,000 this month, then you just simply apply the formula which will result to the amounts below.

   $70,000 = $100,000 – $20,000 – $10,000

   That means that you have $70,000 spendable amount that you can work on a budget.

1. *From the spendable amount, subtract the fixed obligations*

   Fixed obligations pertain to the amount that must be paid every month. It includes house rental, amortisation of car mortgage, and payments to be set aside for other bills. It takes priority in your budget because it must be paid no matter what.

2. *From the rest of the spendable amount, subtract the other expenses*

   Once you have deducted the fixed obligations from the spendable amount, the next step would be to identify and allot a budget for other expenses. An envelope method is useful for this. Using this method, you will prepare a number of envelopes with the particular amount of money that is set aside for it. It could be for food, allowances of children, and even a small portion that will go to your fund to purchase a new refrigerator set.

   The key to maximizing this budget and reaping the rewards is to stick to it. There might be some times when you are tempted to go over the amount that is set aside in a particular envelope, but just remember to honor your agreement with your spouse and think about the goal of why you are doing this.

Need VS Want

To spend your money wisely, you need to have a thorough system to identify whether a particular expense is just a want or a genuine need. Most people fall into the trap of spending their money on things that they want rather those things that they really need.

For instance, you are walking inside a mall then you catch a glimpse of the latest LCD TV model. The picture is so vivid that you just can't take your eyes off it. You look at the price and learn that you have enough money to make the purchase. However, you also remembered that you just purchased a new LCD TV last year and it still works fine. On this occasion, we can easily conclude that you don't really need the TV, you just want it. You can still make the purchase, but think about the implications of your decision.

Conserve Without Hurting Yourself

Though I am advocating that spouses should learn how to conserve their finances and handle their money in the right way, I do not encourage you to keep the good things from your marriage at all. You might have $1 million dollar deposit in your savings account, but if the cost of that huge amount is that you and your spouse are not able to enjoy your married life to the fullest, then there is still something wrong. A balancing act must be made. Don't forget to include leisure in your budget and as long that you are living within your means, then you will enjoy the company of each other while still making sure to reap the rewards of your labour in the future.

Reflection Questions:

This portion of each chapter aims to help you and your spouse to properly evaluate the principles and concepts that you have learned. Try to answer all the questions truthfully. Discuss it with your spouse so you can gain a greater insight when it comes to your partner's ideas and personal thoughts. It will also be helpful if you could share your answers with another couple who might be delighted to go in the journey with you.

1. How often do you argue when it comes to money? The way you handle your finances does it help you and your spouse to be more satisfied with your marriage? What specific actions can you take to ensure that you don't spend too much time in discussing money management instead of focusing on other important things?

_____

_____

_____

2. Do you usually use your credit card or even apply for a loan in making purchases? Based on your honest perception of yourself, do you still live beneath your means or your actions show that you are not contented with what you have? What is your usual motive when it comes to spending? Do you use your money for the mutual benefit of you and your spouse or you spend it exclusively for your own happiness?

_____

_____

_____

3. Do you use a budget when it comes to handling your finances? If yes, do you see your budget helping you in managing your finances better? How often do you find yourself wanting to go beyond the budget that you have set for a particular expense?

WHAT CAN I DO TO MAKE MY MARRIAGE WORK?

How do you handle it? Consider the purchases that you made over the last six months. List down all the major expenses that you made and identify whether it was a need or a want.

_____

_____

_____

NINTH CRITERION: CULTIVATING THE CONFESSION FACTOR

CHAPTER 11

"The bitterest truth is better than the sweetest lies."

– Michael Stulhbarg

Psychologist Sidney Jourard, in his book *Transparent Self,* revealed some fascinating research and studies about the subject of self-disclosure. One of the major findings that he discussed in the book is the natural inclination and tendency of human to reveal itself. It means that every person has this drive and inner desire to disclose his true personality to another person. However, when this desire is stifled and the individual chose to build walls around himself, then emotional difficulties will result.

Jourard says, *"I wondered whether there was some connection between their reluctance to be known by spouse, family, and friends, and their need to consult with a professional psychotherapist."* The psychologist is hinting of the possibility of contacting serious problems, issues and even mental and physical sickness when walls are built to keep other persons out.

The same notion can also be said when it comes to marital relationships. When a spouse chose to be dishonest, keep secrets, and wear a mask in front of his or her spouse, then problems are bound to come in the relationship. Choosing to hide your true personality, thoughts, and emotions might absolve a person of handling the pressure at the moment, but it will never go away. It will accumulate until there is no way to go and all the secrets that were kept will explode and damage the relationship forever.

In this chapter, we will discuss the art of self-disclosure, how to facilitate openness and cultivate the confession factor when it comes to marital relationships. We will also elaborate on the different benefits that confession and openness can give for you and your spouse. And lastly, I will give you some practical tips and insights on how you can utilize the art of disclosing yourself to one another to improve and strengthen your marriage.

The Art of Openness

One of the pillars of great relationships is the pillar of trust. And marriage is not an exception. A person cannot be dishonest and at the same time expect that the relationship with his spouse will remain stable and lasting. Trust is essential in marriage and one of its cornerstones is openness.

Be transparent to your spouse

The idea of transparency brings to mind the image of a clear glass window. When the window is free from smudges and dirt, the person outside can clearly see what is happening inside and vice versa. On the other hand, when the window is full of dirt and just outright filth, seeing the view from both sides will be difficult.

This idea is the same when it comes to marriage. When both spouses are not transparent to each other, there is difficulty in seeing what's really happening inside and thus connection and intimacy will suffer. To be transparent means to be totally clear and open to what is happening inside of you. It is about telling your spouse the things that is swirling around your mind and even the things that are weighing heavily on your heart.

When you are transparent, you remove any barrier that might hinder your partner to see right through you. Instead, you are opening yourself to inquiries and questions that will help your spouse to understand you better.

"Transparency and honesty are key in building more trust in any relationship" Chindah Chindah

Be completely honest with your spouse

In a research conducted by the law firm, Slater & Gordon, the researchers found out that about 20% of married couples hold some secrets that might destroy the marriage if the secrets come out in the open. About 25% of the 2,175 respondents admitted that they have lied about something important while another 42% believe that they won't be caught out. Though it doesn't free them from the guilt feelings associated with their secrets.

There could be a myriad of reasons why couples tend to keep secrets from each other. However, more often than not, keeping secrets will only cause irreparable damage in relationship. Therefore, it is of utmost importance for a couple to be completely honest to their spouse.

The Benefits of Confession and Openness

Try to remember about the early stages of your relationship with your spouse. Try to think back on the memories of your young love. Go back to the things that you did in those early days of your romance. There were a lot of things, right? But I surmise that one of the things that you truly enjoy doing is when you just talk for hours about a lot of things. When both of you opened your deep-seated emotions, fears, and ambitions. And because of that unique transparency, both of you were drawn to each other. That is one of the benefits of confession and openness.

Openness will draw you closer together

We are normally drawn to those people who are completely honest and transparent with us. It's the same with our spouses. Though our modern culture seems to applaud the reclusive and rugged nature of fictional characters like James Bond, at our core, we all desire to find a person who will trust us enough to reveal what's really going on inside them.

There are a lot of reasons why people build elaborate façade and wear masks just to hide their true selves. Perhaps they are afraid of being rejected or judged by others. Or maybe they don't want to reveal the ugly side of themselves – weaknesses, wounds, and embarrassing experiences. This notion is mostly damaging for couples.

Husbands, who usually take pride in their competence, always project their calm demeanor and avoid showing their weaknesses to their spouse. The wives, on the other hand, want transparency from their partners. They need to connect emotionally, but not with the James Bond wall that their husbands have built. However, once this wall and masks are broken, openness and transparency will draw the couples together seeing their mutual need for support from each other.

Openness will give you freedom and security

Couples who have found the courage to be completely transparent to each other can testify about the comforting sense of freedom and security that they found. Nothing is more liberating than knowing that your spouse accepts you for who you are – warts and all. It also provides security, knowing that your partner will readily accept you and won't judge you no matter what kind of emotions you bring to the table.

Think about this. What if you can completely be yourself in front of your spouse? You can show him your weaknesses because you don't need to impress him with your elaborate façade. You can also spill out what's on your mind and what you feel at the moment knowing that there is a loving hand that will accept you for who you are.

George Elliot said it more beautifully. She said, *"Oh the comfort, the inexpressible comfort of feeling safe with a person; having neither to weigh thoughts nor measure words but to pour them all out, just as it is, chaff and grain together, knowing that a faithful hand will take and sift them, keeping what is worth keeping, and then, with the breath of kindness blow the rest away."*

Openness will help you in self-discovery

More often than not, those people who hide their true selves will find themselves not knowing who they really are. They wear their masks to the point that they don't know any more what's true and what's not. This could happen even if you have been married for a long time. Sometimes, we think that it is easier to keep up the pretence instead of going out of the way to reveal what's really going on inside.

For instance, a husband might display the image of a guy who keeps his cool under any circumstance. Whenever his wife would come to him to vent out her fears and frustrations, he would just brush off the issue and calmly say, *"C'mon, honey. It's not that big of a problem. Just chill!"* Will his wife find virtue in this emotionless display of sympathy? I don't think so. But if the husband does this continually, then it would be more difficult for him to show his own fears and frustrations and might end up alienating his true condition.

"Fake it, 'til you make it" is not an ideal concept when it comes to marriage. Instead, try to show who you truly are. And as you become open to your spouse, then it will enable you to learn more about yourself and discover the real strength that might be lying dormant inside you.

Useful Insights in Openness

Though we advocate the virtue of openness and transparency in this chapter, there are still some things that you must consider when applying the principles of confession in your life. Prudence must always be a part of everything that we do including laying out in the open the things that are happening inside us.

Keeping your opinion to yourself

Some people who learnt the principles of openness and confession have the mistaken notion that they should always display candor in all their conversations. However, let's face it. We don't want to talk to a person who always voice out his counter opinions to us. In the same way, we don't want to be around a person who has an opposing thing to say to every matter that will be bring up.

When talking with your spouse, you must also to learn to keep your mouth shut on certain occasions. There are moments when all your partner wants is a person who will listen to his or her qualms. In fact, I would go as far as to say that sometimes, he or she is not asking for your opinion on the matter.

Take hold of your emotions

Have you been with a person who has no restraint when it comes to his or her emotions? Whether he is happy, sad, or angry, he doesn't distinguish on the circumstances but always vent out everything that he feels. However, having no restraint is one sign of a deep psychological problem.

It is important to be completely transparent with your spouse, but you must also learn to express your emotions in a proper way. For instance, you were offended by one of the remarks of your partner while talking with some of your friends. What's the best way to deal with this situation? Would you be completely open and let her know what you feel by walking out? Or would you wait until you get home and share with her what you feel in private? Well, prudence suggests that you should wait and thus, take hold of your emotions for the mean time.

Examine your motives in sharing

Part of being completely honest with your spouse is letting him know about the past mistakes that remained covered up until now. Perhaps you have committed some minor offence like taking $100 from his wallet without his knowing, or maybe a more serious sin like flirting or committing infidelity with your officemate.

This path is genuinely dangerous to cross because it might determine whether the marriage will continue or not. However, what's more important is the motive of why you want to share it with your spouse. Do you want to sincerely let him know that you have committed a serious mistake and ask for his forgiveness? Or you just want to remove the guilt off yourself and pass the buck to your partner?

A good practice before opening up is to reflect on your motives and intentions why you want to do what you intend to do in the first place. It would also be helpful to talk to a trusted friend or counsellor about the matter – just to clear your mind – before disclosing it to your spouse.

Forgive one another

In relation to the process of opening sensitive and damaging secrets, it is of utmost importance that couples be open to reconciliation and forgiveness. There are a lot of reasons why people make mistakes. And whether it is by intent or completely unintentional – a mistake will always be a mistake.

The process of forgiveness and reconciliation will be much easier by having the understanding that both of you have also committed mistakes in the past. No one is perfect. And if you will allow your love to run its course, then it will demand that your genuinely forgive each other and move on towards the future.

Sensitive Transparency

The principle of confession and openness can bring healing and transformation for both of you and for the relationship as well. In fact, the Bible puts a heavy emphasis on the need of confessing sins to one another. James said in his epistles, *"Confess your sins to each other and pray for each other so that you may be healed."* Confession can bring healing to the relationship. However, careless confession might do more harm than good. Therefore, both of you must practise sensitive transparency. Be sensitive to the current circumstance and situation, consider deeply what your spouse might think and feel about you once you confess everything, and lastly, pray about it, especially if the offence is serious enough to threaten the marriage. In the end, practise prudent confession and watch your relationship grow as you live in complete honesty, transparency and openness.

Reflection Questions:

This portion of each chapter aims to help you and your spouse to properly evaluate the principles and concepts that you have learned. Try to answer all the questions truthfully. Discuss it with your spouse so you can gain a greater insight when it comes to your partner's ideas and personal thoughts. It will also be helpful if you could share your answers with another couple who might be delighted to go in the journey with you.

1. On a scale of 1 to 10, with 1 being the lowest and 10 being the highest, how honest are you with your spouse? What kind of secrets do you usually keep from your partner? What do you think is the harm that keeping secrets bring in the relationship? How can you avoid it?

_____

_____

2. Do this separately. List down all the things that you are not yet opening up to your spouse. It might be a fear or phobia that haunted you since childhood or it could be a more serious offence like flirting with another person. Don't leave out anything. After you have written down those things, pray about it and make a concrete plan on how you will disclose it to your spouse.

_____

_____

3. Define openness and transparency in your own words. Do you believe that it is important for married couples to be completely honest with each other? Kindly elaborate your answer. How will you ensure that confession and openness will become a daily part of your relationship?

_____

_____

TENTH CRITERION: NURTURING THE MARRIAGE THROUGH CONTINUATION

CHAPTER 12

"You don't marry one person; you marry three:
the person they think they are, the person they are,
and the person they are going to become as a result
of being married to you."

– *Richard Needham*

There is a growing change in the perception and view of modern scholars about the institution of marriage. Most of them say that marriages, along with the society, are growing more individualistic. They infer that spouses are now living *"alone together."* If this is true, then the state of marriages is truly saddening. An institution that was once celebrated as a blessed union of two souls is now reduced to an agreement in paper to live together under one roof.

Fortunately, a recent study published in the Journal of Family Theory and Review, went against this notion of individualistic marriage. Carrie Yodanis and Sean Lauer, main authors of the research, noted that couples, in spite of the tendency of the society to promote individualism, still chose to live in interdependent partnerships with each other. It is indeed how marriage is supposed to be – a union of two individuals who combine their lives to form a single unit of family.

In addition, it is also essential to mention that in order for marriage to stay, a plan for continuation or improvement must be in place. Individuals do not remain static. Persons change and so do couples. And marriage must also be affected by these changes. In this chapter, we will discuss the different goals of marriage and how couples can achieve those goals in order for their marriage to thrive and grow.

Goals in Marriage

Setting goals is absolutely important in every aspects of life including the arena of marriage. You don't enter into a relationship without any fixed goals in mind because you don't want to waste your time and your life in the arms of somebody who doesn't even know the direction that they are heading to.

In fact, in recent studies and research, it has been continually noted that shared goals are needed for a marriage to last. In a study conducted by the Australian Institute of Family Studies, they concluded that an agreement on aims and goals is one of the main ingredients of marital success. This result was in accordance with what 351 couples said.

There could be a myriad of goals for marital relationship, but I give you the three most important goals that I could think of.

Mutual Growth and Improvement

On Abraham Maslow's *Hierarchy of Needs,* he put the need of self-actualisation as the most important need of humans. Individuals have this inner desire to unleash their potential and make a significant impact in this world. However, in most marriages, the need for self-actualisation is being overshadowed by the problems and issues of a married life.

However, mutual growth and improvement must still be in the top priority of every married couple. Some individuals are driven by their personal growth and improvement and when their spouse do not provide the atmosphere and support to do that, then they are most likely to have friction in their relationship. On the other hand, if the couple mutually agree that they will help each other to become the best version of themselves, then their marriage will be taken to another level. And this level will encourage and aim to fulfil the greatest need of each spouse.

Strong and Loving Family

Another important goal of any married couple is to build a strong and loving family. The Bible says in Malachi 2:15, *"Didn't the LORD make you one with your wife? In body and spirit you are his. And what does He want? Godly children from your union. So guard your heart; remain loyal to the wife of your youth."*

More than enjoying the companionship of each other and basking in the sweetness of your romantic love, your goal should also be to build a family that is intellectually strong, morally upright and emotionally stable. If your marriage right now is not a place where these things are being encouraged, then it's time to make some adjustments and set a goal to produce a stronger and a more loving family.

Healthy Support System

One of the most admirable characteristics of successful marriage is the robust support system that couples provide to each other and to the family as a whole. Your marriage is not a place where you are out to destroy each other. In fact, it must be a place where you work as a team and you support each other's endeavour while making sure that you are acting in the best interest of everyone in the family.

A healthy support system is one where there is no fear of being judged or rejected. It is a place where dreams can thrive and success is highly encouraged. In this kind of marriage, both couples will experience the bliss of reaching new heights individually and collectively as partners.

Achieving Marriage Goals

Setting goals is not the end point, it is just the beginning. And it will not be completed without having the capability to reach it. Marriage must be a place where both persons are growing individually while the relationship is getting deeper day by day. It thrives in the understanding that husband and wife unconditionally accepts each other and help each other to achieve the individual and collective goals. These marital goals will only be achieved through marital teamwork that will result to marital success.

Improve Yourself Individually

In spite of the reality of being married and working on a mutual aim or goal, you can't still deny the fact that both of you are individual persons with their own unique passion, purpose and potential. Thus, it is important that both of you invest time separately on improving and growing yourself individually.

There will be times when you must be separated for a moment so one of you could pursue personal development and improve on what he wants to do. This is perfectly fine and this is the place where the support system of the marriage must function. Improving yourself individually has both individual and collective benefits as well.

Work on Relationship and Keep Learning

Building yourself individually is important, but it is more essential to ensure that your relationship is growing as well. How can you say that your marriage is growing? One way is to examine the problems that you are constantly encountering. When your marriage is thriving, then the level of maturity between you and your spouse is improving. If you have been constantly arguing over simple matters before, but now it is virtually eliminated, then it means that you mature as a couple.

On a more practical note, if you have experienced some major financial problems before because of poor knowledge in money management , but you put in an effort to learn it so that now you don't have any problem when it comes to money, then you have again grown in your relationship. As you can see, the main ingredient here is continuous learning.

Be Stubbornly Intentional

In a research conducted by Galena Rhoades of the University of Denver, they were able to find out that the quality and thought that couples put in their decision making can have a lasting impact on their marriage. Couples who are clearly decisive and intentional when it comes to their marriage are more likely to have better marriages compared to couples who just let their impulses dictate their decisions.

Rhoades wrote, *"Couples who slide through their relationship transitions have poorer marital quality than those who make intentional decisions about major milestones."* If you want to achieve your goals as a couple, then you need to be more intentional in planning and making decisions. And through each goal that you achieve, your sense of accomplishment will be enhanced and the marital satisfaction will deepen.

Goal-Oriented Marriage

If there is one thing that separates the successful and happy marriages from the unsuccessful and failing ones, that is the goals that the couples set for themselves. And admittedly, setting goals and doing your best to achieve them is quite a struggle. It is easier to just plow through life and be carried away by the problems that plagued most marriages and then try to solve all those unending barrage of trials. But there is another way, and that is to set mutual goals and aspirations and support each other to achieve them.

Don't be a part of the statistics of failed marriages. You have the power to take initiative and set goals that both you and your spouse will enjoy achieving. It will strengthen your bond and will also give you the necessary boost to deepen your relationship.

Reflection Questions:

This portion of each chapter aims to help you and your spouse to properly evaluate the principles and concepts that you have learned. Try to answer all the questions truthfully. Discuss it with your spouse so you can gain a greater insight when it comes to your partner's ideas and personal thoughts. It will also be helpful if you could share your answers with another couple who might be delighted to go in the journey with you.

1. What is your current goal in your marriage? What do you think is the importance of agreeing to a particular goal and doing your best as a couple to achieve it?

   _____

   _____

2. What is your usual response when your spouse wants to do something new? Are you an encourager and supporter or you mostly criticise and sow apprehensions? No matter what your response is, how has it been impacting your marriage?

   _____

   _____

3. Can you honestly say that you and your spouse are currently working as a team? Elaborate. Also, what specific goals do you have for yourself? Does it contribute in the fulfilment of your goal as a married couple?

   _____

   _____

   _____

ELEVENTH CRITERION: LIVING IN COMPLETION OF MARRIAGE

CHAPTER 13

"Marriage is the hardest thing you will ever do. The secret is removing divorce as an option. Anybody who gives themselves that option will get a divorce."

– Will Smith

"... for better, for worse, for richer, for poorer, in sickness and in health, until death do us part."

Couples commonly pledge the above vow to their spouse on their wedding day. Considering carefully the words in the vow, you can immediately grasp the context that marriage is made to last and divorce is never an option. However, with the rapidly increasing rate of divorce in different parts of the world, it begs the question whether these words in the wedding vow are just considered a mundane part of the ceremony and not to be taken seriously.

If you have been married for quite a while now then you know the marriage is not supposed to be easy. The notion of *'happily ever after'* does not exist in the real world, because real marriage is messy, painful, and sometimes regretful. Indeed, the words of the marriage vow ring true – worse, poorer, sickness, and sometimes even death. Yet, it is absolutely important that couples decide to hold on to the things that they vowed to each other during their wedding ceremony. It is essential that they do not just speak those words out of tradition but be willing to uphold it all the remaining days of their lives.

WHAT CAN I DO TO MAKE MY MARRIAGE WORK?

So what does it really mean when you say *'till death do us part?'* Is there any special meaning that is attached to it? How should that simple but heavy phrase guide your everyday lives as a married couple?

Stay on Each Other's Side – No Matter What

Let's face it, the circumstances inside marriage are not always favourable to the spouses. There are a lot of problems, trials and conflicts that spouses need to weather through. And this truth poses a significant problem, especially in a generation that wants quick fixes in everything. With the advancement of technology, it is easier to replace a defective appliance instead of taking the pain to repair it. However, this mentality is being dangerously extended even to marital relationships – a relationship that is not meant to be replaced.

When you say *'till death do us part,'* you are saying that you are willing to stay beside your spouse no matter what circumstances come. Indeed, there will be days when all you want to do is to leave him, but because of your vow to be with him until death, then you have to grit your teeth and work together to make the relationship better.

Divorce is Never an Option

Married couples are meant to stay together until one of them draws his or her last breath. Considering this idea then, both of you must remove divorce from your options. There is power in having the resolve to think in this manner. If you remove divorce from your list of alternatives; when the marriage turns sour, then it will also force you to stay and at the same time work out your differences and conflicts.

In fact, marriage experts have found out that those couples who decide to remove divorce from their choices are the same couples who can make their marriage work. With the growing number of couples who are opting to go their separate ways, it is a shame that their main problem started when they left their options open. And when squalls and storms hit their relationship, they see divorce as an easy way to escape the pain and feel happiness once again. But does divorce really make individuals happy?

In a research conducted by the Institute for American Values, they discovered the following findings that debunked the myth of happiness after divorce:

- Unhappy married couples who chose to get divorced were no happier on the average, compared to unhappy married couples who chose to stay married.
- Choosing to stay married did not normally trap unhappy spouses in violent relationships.
- 2 out of 3 unhappy married couples who avoided divorce or separation ended up happy in their marriage after five years.

As you can see, with the tenacity to stay in the relationship and the drive to make things better, things indeed get better for their marriage.

Focus on Each Other's Strength and Not Pique on Weaknesses

One reason why marriages turn sour is the tendency of couples to resent each other and highlight each other's weaknesses. There is definitely a time when you will have a keen eye to see the imperfections of your spouse. This is during the time when the chemicals of romantic love in the body have waned. During this period, the flaws and mistakes of your spouse will be magnified and sometimes you just can't help but to notice it and nag your partner about it and vice versa.

However, this is a foolhardy way to live with your spouse. It's difficult to live in a painful contest of whose better and who's the loser while trying to love each other in a more meaningful and deeper way. So instead of thinking about how you could criticise your spouse, why not focus on each other's strength. Encourage your partner in those areas where he is genuinely skilful and consistently give some words of affirmation. This will not just boost the self-confidence of your spouse but will also see you in a better light. Who wouldn't want someone beside him that always sees the best in him?

Make a Plan for Your Marriage

Marriage is a complex relationship. No one can have marital success without having the proper planning and setting of some goals for their relationship. The other side of the vow, *"... better, richer, health"* can only be achieved by adding planning to your marriage activities. Create a plan on how you can become better as individual persons and as couple. Do you need to read books or attend a seminar? How can you become richer as a couple? And how can you protect the health of each other? These things need intricate planning and faithful execution from both of you.

That's what it means to have that kind of marriage where only death can separate both of you. In a basketball, the team might have talented players but without the guidance of the coach and team work, the team won't still win. It's the same with marriage. You might be amazing individuals separately, but how about as a couple? Do you still shine? Create a plan, listen to other people who are ahead of you in their marriage, and work as a team.

Seek Professional Help if Needed

Most people wear their pride as if it is a necklace that they should be proud of. But most of the time, their pride becomes the leading cause of their destruction. It's the same with marriage. It would be great if you could deal with your own problems, and come up with a resolution that will lead you to love each other even more. But if you can't handle the problem on your own, then there is nothing wrong in seeking professional help.

In fact, in a research conducted by the American Association of Marriage and Family Therapists, they concluded that couples and family who have tried counselling and therapy sessions are highly satisfied with what they have received. Over 98% said that they received good or excellent couples counselling while 97% of respondents said that they got the help that they needed.

Making Your Marriage Last

With the ever increasing propensity of people for quick fixes, the rate of divorce will just keep increasing if not remain constant. This could be alarming especially for newly wed couples. However, as stated at the beginning chapter, there is a simple way to counteract this and that is to remove divorce from your options. You can try talking it out, making a plan for your marriage and even seeking professional help – but never consider divorcing your spouse or get separated. Think about this. Whether you continue in your marriage or end up in divorce, you will both experience pain – The pain of working out your marriage, and the pain of destroying your vow to your spouse and for your family. You can make your marriage last, but that will be based on the choices that you make today.

"For your marriage to work, you must be obsess with the principles and guidelines of a successful marriage" Chindah Chindah

Reflection Questions:

This portion of each chapter aims to help you and your spouse to properly evaluate the principles and concepts that you have learned. Try to answer all the questions truthfully. Discuss it with your spouse so you can gain a greater insight when it comes to your partner's ideas and personal thoughts. It will also be helpful if you could share your answers with another couple who might be delighted to go in the journey with you.

1. Do you still consider divorce as one of the options in your marriage? Kindly explain your answer. What do you think is the effect of having the mentality that divorce is one of the options that you can use to escape the pain and to achieve happiness?

_____

_____

_____

2. Do you know people in your circle that have experienced divorce? If yes, then try to interview him or her and ask whether the divorce results in a greater happiness to his life? If he or she is still willing to share, ask if there is anything that he or she regrets.

_____

_____

3. During those conflicted times in your marriage, what is your usual way of overcoming the problem? Who are the persons that you approach to help you in your problem? Do you believe that having counselling sessions is helpful for your marriage? Why or why not?

_____

_____

TWELFTH CRITERION:
HAVING DIVINE CONSCIOUSNESS

CHAPTER 14

"Therefore what God has joined together, let not man separate."

– Matthew 19:6

In an age where a lot of couples are getting divorced and marriages are turning into a wreck, asking the question of the secret to make marriages satisfying and lasting is important more than ever. In several studies published in the Journal of Family Psychology, the researchers concluded that cultivating practices such as praying selfless prayer, deepening spiritual intimacy and building compassionate love can help couples to withstand the challenges of a married life – from the early stages, to becoming parents and even during old age. In another study published in Sociology of Religion, the researchers found out that couples who have made their faith a priority and married for religious reasons are less likely to commit the sin of adultery.

All these studies speak of one important fact. Having God at the centre of your relationship as a couple is essential to keeping your marriage healthy and to enable you have the strength to withstand the trials and problems that might come in your marital relationship. Think about this. If you have faith in God that makes you to have hope and His eternal words and you follow what the Bible says in 1 Corinthians 13, then what do you think will happen in your relationship? If you apply what the Bible teaches about forgiveness and loving other people as you love yourself, will your marriage become stronger? If you submit to each other just like what the

Bible teaches in Ephesians, will you love each other in a deeper way? The bible has spoken about what most renowned family psychologist, philosophers and therapist are offering as keys to building a happy relationship.

God invented marriage and He is the One who has the perfect knowledge to make your marriage like it's supposed to be – edifying, satisfying and lasting. Even, if you don't believe in God, you can at least follow his marriage principles and see if he means the worse or the best for your relationship. In this chapter, we will examine the concept of putting God in the centre of your relationship if you believe and you are willing to allow Him to get involved in your relationship. We will also look at the different ways that you and your spouse can practise to have a more God-centered marriage. And lastly, we will evaluate your need for God in different stages of your marital relationship.

A Picture of God-centred Marriage

If you are a person of faith, I know that you already have an idea of the need to put God in the centre of your relationship. However, if you still don't have any idea what it means to have God take charge in your relationship, then I hope that you would continue reading with me. Though, the principles that you are about to learn are found in the Bible, I firmly believe that these concepts can still help you to protect, save and improve your marriage.

Seek God's Divine Help and Guidance

Putting God in the centre of your marriage simply means that you let God and His Words be the guide in the decisions that you make with regards to your relationship. In other words, you will use the Bible as a standard in the way you live as husband and wife. It is about having the consciousness and divine perspective that God wants to help you in the challenges that you face in your marriage.

We have the tendency to tackle issues on our own. And when there is nothing that we can do, we are forced to just put the matter in the hands of God as the last resort. But why not try it the other way round? Instead of putting God the last of your list of sources of help, why not put Him first? When you are undergoing a problem, pray and ask for His help and guidance of what you should do. The first avenue that He can talk to you are through the Bible. It will also be helpful to find someone who is spiritually mature and ask for godly wisdom in dealing with your problems.

Connect with God Spiritually and with Each Other

They say that the best relationships are those that consist of three persons, you, your spouse, and God at the centre. Connecting with God will bring you and your partner closer. When both of you are also in a relationship with the Lord, and you are faithful to follow His words, then you can strengthen your marriage in ways that you can never imagine.

Let us try with this passage that is found in Paul's epistle to the Ephesian church. Read carefully through these verses and imagine the benefits that your marriage can get when you live according to these words from the Bible:

"Submit to one another out of reverence for Christ. Wives, submit to your own husbands as you do to the Lord... Husbands, love your wives, just as Christ loved the church and gave himself up for her... each one of you also must love his wife as he loves himself, and the wife must respect her husband." (Ephesians 5:21, 22, 25, 33)

When you are connected spiritually to God, your marriage will take on a new level. Yes, there will still be challenges and a lot of bumps along the way. But your connection with the source of love and power will help you to become more connected as you face and overcome each challenge.

Pray as a couple

Have you already practised praying with your spouse together? I know it might feel awkward at first talking to God about the deepest things inside your heart while your spouse is right there beside you hearing everything that you are saying. However, praying with your spouse is one of the most romantic activities that you can do. In addition to your transparency, you are also allowing your spouse to hear how much you care for him while praying. Also, prayer can be a deterrent for heated arguments. Besides, how can you pray with someone who you are angry with?

While praying as a couple, remember to pray not just for the wellbeing of each other but also about the struggles and challenges that your spouse might be facing right now. It will also be encouraging to pray that she will become the person that God meant her to be. They say that couples who pray together stay together. I sincerely believe in that.

The Need for God in Marriage

As of this moment, I hope you don't have the mistaken notion that you only need God in your relationship when the going gets tough. It is easy to fall into the trap of thinking that God is only concerned in your relationship when there are challenges and problems because He can show His power during this time. However, the Lord is concerned with every aspect and every season of your relationship. In fact, He wants to be involved in your marriage at every step of the way.

At the beginning of your marriage

During the early stages of your marriage, your strong love for each other might be an essential factor to stay together. But as you already know, the love chemicals in our body that is responsible in releasing the intoxicating feeling of being in-love won't last. At this moment, God can help you in sustaining your love even if you are now noticing a lot of annoying characteristics of your spouse.

When your spouse is doing a lot of things to make you angry, you can remind yourself what the Bible says in Colossians 3:13, *"Make allowance for each other's fault, and forgive anyone who offends you. Remember, the Lord forgave you, so you must forgive others."* Also, at the beginning of your marriage, you need the wisdom to navigate through the unfamiliar waters of marital relationship, and again, God can help you with that. He is the Author of marriage and He can show you the right way towards marital success.

In the middle of your marriage

Having your own family and taking care of your children is a tough job for any individuals. Studies show that marital satisfaction starts decreasing when children arrive in the lives of married couples. Also, the task of nurturing and raising a child is also challenging as it gets. The good thing is that the Word of God provide wisdom to handle this kind of situation in your marriage.

For instance, when it comes to discipline and raising your child, the Bible says in Proverbs 22:6, *"Direct your children onto the right path, and when they are older, they will not leave it."* In another verse, Ephesians 6:4 says, *"Fathers, do not provoke your children to anger; instead, bring them up in the discipline and instruction of the Lord."*

At the end of your marriage

The wedding vow says, *'till death do us part.'* Death is a reality of life. You might want to escape it but you can't. And sometimes, this might be the cause of the end of your marriage. It is hard to comprehend why God would allow our spouses to die and leave us. And to be honest, I don't have an answer either. But what we do have is the promise of eternal life for those who believe in the Name of Jesus.

And if it will provide comfort, here is what Paul said in 1 Thessalonians 4:16 – 18, *"For the Lord himself will descend from heaven with a cry of command, with the voice of an archangel, and with the sound of the trumpet of God. And the dead in Christ will rise first. Then we who are alive, who are left, will be caught up together with them in the clouds to meet the Lord in the air, and so we will always be with the Lord. Therefore encourage one another with these words."*

Divine Consciousness to a Lasting Marriage

God only wants what is best for us – even in our marriage. If your marriage is currently undergoing some kind of trouble, then be encouraged with the truth that God is the author of marriage and He has a beautiful plan for your relationship. You just need to have a Divine Consciousness and understand that God wants to be the centre of your relationship. Connect with the Lord. Learn from His Words. Pray together as a couple. And watch as He takes your relationship from rock bottom to the high heavens of marital satisfaction and success. He can do that and He is willing to do it because He is good!

"God plays a huge role in any marriage that feels He is important" Chindah Chindah

Reflection Questions:

This section of each chapter aims to help you and your spouse to properly evaluate the principles and concepts that you have learned. Try to answer all the questions truthfully. Discuss it with your spouse so you can gain a greater insight when it comes to your partner's ideas and personal thoughts. It will also be helpful if you could share your answers with another couple who might be delighted to go in the journey with you.

1. On a scale of 1 to 10, with 10 being the highest and 1 being the lowest, what's the status of your marriage in terms of your relationship with God? Do you think that your faith and level of spirituality has any relevance when it comes to marital success? Why or why not?

    _____

    _____

    _____

2. What specific ways can you adopt to make sure that God will be the centre of your relationship? How can you connect more spiritually to God and with each other? Get a Bible and read through the passages mentioned in this chapter and reflect on what God is saying to you.

    _____

    _____

    _____

3. In what stage of marriage are you currently? What kind of problems are you currently experiencing right that might need divine help and guidance from the Lord?

    _____

    _____

EPILOGUE

"The greatest marriages are built on teamwork. A mutual respect, a healthy dose of admiration, and a never-ending portion of love and grace."

– Fawn Weaver

Congratulations on reaching the end of this book. I sincerely hope that you enjoyed reading it as much as I enjoyed writing it to help you in building a lasting marriage that most people only dreamed of. It has always been my utmost desire to see the kind of marriage that people will be proud of, to look at couples who see past their differences and flaws while fixing their gaze on the qualities that they admire in each other, and to prove to the world that a happy marriage can be the rule and not the exception. Through this book, I believe that I have given my share – no matter how insignificant it is – in the fulfilment of that dream.

In spite of that noble intention to contribute to the happiness of marriage on this planet, one of the things that I carefully considered when I was writing this book is the sheer number of principles and concepts that I want to teach you. The Twelve, as we call it in this book, can be a daunting list for others that will just paralyse them into inaction. For some, it might be just another to-do-list and self-help motivational talk but won't still suffice to implement lasting change. There might be also some individuals who might follow the practical tips and advice, yet still feel so far from their spouse because they do it grudgingly. I hope that those things will not happen to you.

Let me reiterate once again my suggested strategies to make sure that you will make the most of this book.

EPILOGUE

1. Read the book from start to finish getting a general feel of what the book is all about. It will also be helpful if you will take note of the different sections of the book, or get a highlighter to mark those words, phrases, and paragraphs that communicate with you at a much deeper level. If you are already married, then it will be wise to do the initial reading separately, thus giving you the time and space that you need to reflect on the things that you are learning.

2. After the initial reading, go through the book once again, but this time make it a little slower than the first reading. The goal of the second reading is to engage your mind and heart in a more profound manner, thus revealing those specific areas that need to be covered and worked on. If you already have a spouse, then it would also be ideal that you discuss from time to time the concepts that you have learnt and how it can apply to your relationship.

3. During the second reading, you will gain some valuable insights on the different aspects of your relationship that need major overhaul. You might also notice that you are working great in other areas while failing miserably to deliver in other areas. That is perfectly normal. What I suggest is that you rank the Twelve based on the worst criterion to the good ones.

4. After ranking the Twelve based on the urgency and importance (*worst to good),* now it's time to work and cultivate your relationship starting with the worst aspect. Spend a month on each aspect until you cover all Twelve. During this period, you can also read other books and consult with other experts in that specific aspect. Repeat the process until you are comfortable enough with the Twelve.

Marriage is supposed to last a lifetime. In the same way, working on your marriage is also supposed to last until both of you draw your last breath. To be totally honest with you, I believe that the entire details of marriage concepts and principles could not be totally taught in just one book. The dynamics of marital relationship, the intricacies of human interactions, and the complexities of having children all add up to create the beautiful union that we call *"marriage."*

Now, my friend, this book is not the end. In fact, this might just be the beginning. And just like any other books that you will pick up to read, what matters most is not the things that you know in your head, but the things you embrace in your heart and apply in your life. Go on. Read. Apply. But don't forget to embrace your partner like the first time that you hug each other. It's not about what you know that matters, it's about the sincere desire to work towards building that foundation – the true foundation of lasting marriage.

KEYNOTES

Introduction

1. "Marriage and Divorce Statistics." *ec.europa.eu.* Last modified December 22, 2016. http://ec.europa.eu/eurostat/statistics-explained/index.php/Marriage_and_divorce_statistics

2. Claire Cain Miller. "The Divorce Surge is Over, but the Myth Lives On." *The New York Times.* Last modified December 2, 2014. https://www.nytimes.com/2014/12/02/upshot/the-divorce-surge-is-over-but-the-myth-lives-on.html?smid=fb-nytimes&smtyp=cur&bicmp=AD&bicmlukp=WT.mc_id&bicmst=1409232722000&bicmet=1419773522000&_r=3&abt=0002&abg=0

Chapter 1

1. Gretchen Livingston and Andrea Caumont. "5 Facts On Love and Marriage in America." *Pew Research.* Last modified February 13, 2017. http://www.pewresearch.org/fact-tank/2017/02/13/5-facts-about-love-and-marriage/

2. Tom W. Smith, Jaesok Son, and Benjamin Schapiro. "General Social Survey: Trends in Psychological Well-Being, 1972-2014." Presentation by the NORC at the University of Chicago, Chicago, IL, April, 2015.

3. K. Daniel O'Leary, Bianca P. Acevedo, Arthur Aron, Leonie Huddy, and Debra Mashek. "Is Long-Term Love More Than A Rare Phenomenon? If So, What Are Its Correlates?" *Social Pyschological and Personality Science* 3, no. 2 (2012). Accessed March 8, 2017. http://journals.sagepub.com/doi/pdf/10.1177/19485506114170

15

4. Bella M. DePaulo, Deborah A. Kashy, Susan E. Kirkendol, Melissa M. Wver, and Jennifer A. Epstein. "Lying in everyday life." *Journal of Personality and Social Psychology* 70, no. 5 (1996). Accessed March 8, 2017. http://dx.doi.org/10.1037/0022-3514.70.5.979

5. Daily Mail Reporter. "Had a row with your partner today? That'll be one of the 2,455 you will have this year." *Daily Mail.* Last modified May 20, 2011. http://www.dailymail.co.uk/news/article-1389002/Fallout-Couples-argue-average-seven-times-day.html

6. Daisy Dumas. "The couple that argues together stays together: How bickering could be the key to a long and healthy marriage." *Daily Mail.* Last modified January 30, 2012. http://www.dailymail.co.uk/femail/article-2094068/The-couple-argues-stays-How-bickering-key-long-healthy-marriage.html

7. John M. Gottman and Robert W. Levenson. "The Timing of Divorce: Predicting When a Couple Will Divorce Over a 14-Year Period." *Journal of Marriage and the Family* 62 (2000). Accessed March 8, 2017. http://ift-malta.com/wp-content/uploads/2013/01/gottman-predictor-of-divorce.pdf

8. Brian D. Doss, Galena K. Rhoades, Scott M. Stanley, Howard J. Markman. "The effect of transition to parenthood on relationship quality: An 8-year prospective study." *Journal of Personality and Social Psychology 96,* no. 3 (2009). Accessed March 8, 2017. https://www.ncbi.nlm.nih.gov/pmc/articles/PMC2702669/

9. Alabama Physicians For Life, Inc. (APFLI). "Couples Living Together Before Marriage Less Likely to Get Married Than Ever: Study." *Physicians for Life.* Last modified May 18, 2015. http://www.physiciansforlife.org/couples-living-together-before-marriage-less-likely-to-get-married-than-ever-study-2015/

Chapter 2

1. Sameen. "25 Biological Differences Between Men and Women That Aren't Commonly Known." *List 25.* Last modified August 29, 2016. http://list25.com/25-biological-differences-between-men-and-women/5/

2. Gregory L. Jantz. "Brain Differences Between Genders." *Psychology Today.* Last modified February 27, 2-14. https://www.psychologytoday.com/blog/hope-relationships/201402/brain-differences-between-genders

3. Spalek, Klara, Matthias Fastenrath, Sandra Ackermann, Bianca Auschra, David Coynel, Julia Frey, Leo Gschwind et al. "Sex-dependent dissociation between emotional appraisal and memory: A large-scale behavioral and fMRI study." *Journal of Neuroscience* 35, no. 3 (2015): 920-935. Accessed March 14, 2017. https://doi.org/10.1523/JNEUROSCI.2384-14.2015

Chapter 3

1. Karney, Benjamin R., and Thomas N. Bradbury. "The longitudinal course of marital quality and stability: A review of theory, methods, and research." *Psychological bulletin* 118, no. 1 (1995): 3. Accessed March 22, 2017. http://psycnet.apa.org/doi/10.1037/0033-2909.118.1.3

2. Arielle Kuperberg. "Does Premarital Cohabitation Raise Your Risk of Divorce?" *Council on Contemporary Families.* Last modified March 10, 2014. https://contemporaryfamilies.org/cohabitation-divorce-brief-report/

3. Laurie DeRose, Mark Lyons-Amos, W. Bradford Wilcox, Gloria Huarcaya. "The Cohabitation-Go-Round: Cohabitation And Family Instability Across the Globe." *Social Trends Institute* (2017). Accessed April 4, 2017. http://marriagefoundation.org.uk/wp-content/uploads/2017/02/WFM-2017-Essay-Embargo.pdf

4. Manning, Wendy D., and Pamela J. Smock. "Measuring and modeling cohabitation: New perspectives from qualitative

data." *Journal of marriage and family* 67, no. 4 (2005): 989-1002. Accessed April 4, 2017.
http://www.bgsu.edu/content/dam/BGSU/college-of-arts-and-sciences/center-for-family-and-demographic-research/documents/working-papers/2004/CFDR-Working-Paper-2004-10-Measuring-and-Modeling-Cohabitation-New-Perspectives-from-Qualitative-Data.pdf

Chapter 4

1. Rochelle Bilow. "Want Your Marriage to Last?" *Your Tango.* Last modified November 18, 2013.
http://www.yourtango.com/experts/rochelle-bilow/want-your-marriage-last

2. Easterling, Beth, David Knox, and Alora Brackett. "Secrets in Romantic Relationships: Does Sexual Orientation Matter?." *Journal of GLBT Family Studies* 8, no. 2 (2012): 196-208. Accessed April 3, 2017.
http://www.tandfonline.com/doi/abs/10.1080/1550428X.2011.623928

3. Burleson, Brant R., and Wayne H. Denton. "The relationship between communication skill and marital satisfaction: Some moderating effects." *Journal of Marriage and the Family* (1997): 884-902. Accessed April 3, 2017.
http://www.jstor.org/stable/35379

Chapter 5

1. Laner, Mary Riege, and J. Neil Russell. "Course content and change in students: Are marital expectations altered by marriage education?." *Teaching Sociology* (1994): 10-18. Accessed April 7, 2017. http://www.jstor.org/stable/1318606

2. Rios, Cicile M. "The relationship between premarital advice, expectations and marital satisfaction." (2010). *All Graduate Theses and Dissertations.* Paper 536. Accessed April 7, 2017. http://digitalcommons.usu.edu/cgi/viewcontent.cgi?article=1532&context=etd

3. Johnson, Kristina D. "Marital Expectation Fulfillment and its

Relationship to Height of Marital Expectations, Optimism, and Relationship Self-Efficacy Among Married Individuals." (2015). *Dissertations.* Paper 1573. Accessed April 7, 2017. http://digitalcommons.andrews.edu/cgi/viewcontent.cgi?article =2823&context=dissertations

Chapter 6

1. Carrere, Sybil, Kim T. Buehlman, John M. Gottman, James A. Coan, and Lionel Ruckstuhl. "Predicting marital stability and divorce in newlywed couples." *Journal of Family Psychology* 14, no. 1 (2000): 42. Accessed April 7, 2017. https://www.researchgate.net/profile/James_Coan/publication/1 2574995_Predicting_marital_stability_and_divorce_in_newly wed_couples/links/0fcfd502d5e84c0980000000.pdf

2. Losada, Marcial, and Emily Heaphy. "The role of positivity and connectivity in the performance of business teams: A nonlinear dynamics model." *American Behavioral Scientist* 47, no. 6 (2004): 740-765. Accessed April 7, 2017. http://www.factorhappiness.at/downloads/quellen/S8_Losada.p df

Chapter 7

1. Birditt, Kira S., Edna Brown, Terri L. Orbuch, and Jessica M. McIlvane. "Marital conflict behaviors and implications for divorce over 16 years." *Journal of Marriage and Family* 72, no. 5 (2010): 1188-1204. Accessed April 8, 2017. Doi:10.1111/j.1741-3737.2010.00758.x

2. McNulty, James K., and V. Michelle Russell. "When "negative" behaviors are positive: A contextual analysis of the long-term effects of problem-solving behaviors on changes in relationship satisfaction." *Journal of personality and social psychology* 98, no. 4 (2010): 587. Accessed April 8, 2017. https://dx.doi.org/10.1037%2Fa0017479

3. Orbuch, Terri L., José A. Bauermeister, Edna Brown, and Brandy Dior McKinley. "Early family ties and marital stability over 16 years: The context of race and gender." *Family relations*

62, no. 2 (2013): 255-268. Accessed April 8, 2017.
https://dx.doi.org/10.1111%2Ffare.12005

Chapter 8

1. Diane Coutu. "Making Relationships Work." *Harvard Business Review.* Last modified December 2007.
https://hbr.org/2007/12/making-relationships-work

2. Galena K. Rhoades and Scott M. Stanley. "Before 'I Do': What Do Premarital Experiences Have to Do with Marital Quality Among Today's Young Adults?" *The National Marriage Project.* The University of Virginia. 2014. Accessed April 16, 2017. http://before-i-do.org/

3. Elizabeth Mitchell. "The Relationship Benefits of a Couples Massage." *The Fashion Spot.* Last modified September 4, 2013.
http://www.thefashionspot.com/life/328285-the-relationship-benefits-of-a-couples-massage/

4. Grover, Shawn, and John F. Helliwell. *How's life at home? New evidence on marriage and the set point for happiness.* No. w20794. National Bureau of Economic Research, 2014. Accessed April 16, 2017.

   http://www.unav.edu/matrimonioyfamilia/observatorio/uploads/32658_NBER_wp20794.pdf

Chapter 9

1. Smith, Tom W. "Adult sexual behavior in 1989: Number of partners, frequency of intercourse and risk of AIDS." *Family planning perspectives* (1991): 102-107. Accessed April 17, 2017. 10.2307/2135820

2. Suzanne Wright. "365 Days of Sex: Can It Strengthen a Marriage?" *Web MD.*
http://www.webmd.com/sex-relationships/features/365-nights-of-sex-can-it-strengthen-a-marriage#1

3. Sheri Stritof. "Why You Should Have Sex More Often." *The Spruce.* Last modified December 23, 2016.
https://www.thespruce.com/why-to-have-sex-more-often-2300937

4. "Couples Who Have Sex Weekly Are Happiest." *Society for Personal and Social Psychology.* Last modified November 17, 2015.
http://www.spsp.org/news-center/press-releases/sex-frequency-study

Chapter 10

1. SunTrust Banks, Inc. "Love and Money: People Say They Save, Partner Spends, According to SunTrust Survey." *PR Newswire.* Last modified February 4, 2015.
http://www.prnewswire.com/news-releases/love-and-money-people-say-they-save-partner-spends-according-to-suntrust-survey-300030921.html

Chapter 11

1. Transparent Self, Sidney Jourard
2. Taryn Hillin. "Survey Says 1 In 5 People Are Keeping A Major Secret From Their Spouse." *The Huffington Post.* Last modified August 1, 2014.
http://www.huffingtonpost.com/2014/08/01/secrets-survey-_n_5642818.html

Chapter 12

1. Yodanis, Carrie, and Sean Lauer. "Is marriage individualized? What couples actually do." *Journal of Family Theory & Review* 6, no. 2 (2014): 184-197. Accessed April 18, 2017.
https://doi/10.1111/jftr.12038
2. Lauer, Robert H., and Jeanette C. Lauer. "Factors in long-term marriages." *Journal of Family Issues* 7, no. 4 (1986): 382-390. Accessed April 18, 2017.
http://journals.sagepub.com/doi/abs/10.1177/019251386007004003
3. Stanley, Scott M., Galena Kline Rhoades, and Howard J. Markman. "Sliding versus deciding: Inertia and the premarital cohabitation effect." *Family Relations* 55, no. 4 (2006): 499-

509. Accessed April 18, 2017.
http://onlinelibrary.wiley.com/doi/10.1111/j.1741-
3729.2006.00418.x/abstract

Chapter 13

1. Waite, Linda J., Don Browning, William J. Doherty, Maggie
    Gallagher, Ye Luo, and Scott M. Stanley. "Does divorce make
    people happy? Findings from a study of unhappy marriages."
    Institute for American Values 4, no. 11 (2002). Accessed April
    19, 2017.
    http://americanvalues.org/catalog/pdfs/does_divorce_make_pe
    ople_happy.pdf
2. "Marriage and Family Therapist: The Family-Friendly Mental
    Health Professionals," Accessed April 19, 2017. http://aamft.org

Chapter 14

1. Mahoney, Annette, and Annmarie Cano. "Introduction to the
    special section on religion and spirituality in family life:
    delving into relational spirituality for couples." *Journal of
    Family Psychology* 28, no. 5 (2014): 583. Accessed April 19,
    2017. http://psycnet.apa.org/doi/10.1037/fam0000030
2. Mahoney, Annette. "Marriage and Family, Faith, and
    Spirituality among Emerging Adults." (2014). Accessed April
    19, 2017.
    http://www.faithformationlearningexchange.net/uploads/5/2/4/
    6/5246709/marriage_and_family_among_emerging_adults_-
    _mahoney.pdf

THE **POWER** OF PERSONAL CHANGE

The Power Of Personal Change
Paperback ISBN:978-0-9957670-1-0
Hardcopy ISBN: 978-0-9957670-0-3

Audiobook Version
Digital ISBN: 9780995767034
Digital Library ISBN: 9780995767041

What would it be like to reach your full potential—to discover what you are truly capable of?

Inside each of us lurks untapped possibility. You are able to change your life, to embark on new and power-inducing habits, and to reach your goals just by making the conscious decision to take a new path.

In this invaluable guide, well-researched concepts and techniques reveal how to reach new levels of success. The key is *embracing change*. Do so effectively, and you can begin pursuing your passions—and achieving goals you've only dreamed about.

Start now! Once you identify your personal strengths, this three-pronged approach will help you determine which goals to pursue and how to get there, step by exciting step.

The difference between average lives and extraordinary ones is not all that great. Give yourself a small push and approach a new era—one consisting of unbounded accomplishment.

Also, connect with Chindah Chindah on your favourite social media platform.

 chindahchindah,F-limitlesslifepro t/chindahchindah
Intag/chindahchindah Youtube/chindah chindah

 https://www.spreaker.com/show/relationship-restoration-reset

 www.limitlesslifepro.com or www.chindahchindah.com or www.4xlpublishing.com

SAVE YOUR MARRIAGE DAILY

Soon to-be-published book.

Are you willing to learn what it takes to save your marriage daily from collapsing?

Or

Are you leaving the saving of your marriage by chance without any decisive effort and commitment?

Marriage is a mystery with unique challenges, which makes it complex but rewardable with the right knowledge and personal effort to make it work.

Men and women perceive emotion, communication, intimacy, fidelity, work and money differently because of the way they were socialized and the ways their parent's perceptions have shaped them over the years. They bring these ideas into the marriage and hence have their own baggage of beliefs regarding what is tolerable and intolerable in a marriage, what they must give to their spouse and what to expect in return.

However, it takes practice to learn that gender differences do not constitute threats to a marriage, but a cause for celebration and an opportunity to expand an individual's sphere of experience. Try to remember that your partner is not your mirror image. In a loving, effective partnership, individuality and separateness are wholesome concepts that each spouse must work at.

Without the awareness that we're supposed to be different, men and women are at odds with one another. We commonly get angry or disappointed with the opposite sex, as we have blocked this crucial reality. We expect the opposite sex to be more like ourselves. We want them to "want what we want" and "believe the way we believe".

We erroneously assume that if our mates love us they'll respond and behave in particular ways—the ways we respond and act when we love somebody. This position sets us up to be frustrated over and over and keeps us from taking the necessary time to communicate lovingly about our differences.

This book is practical, easy to read and will navigate you through realistic and common challenges facing marriages today. So, as to know how to deal with each issue when it arises and to teach you how to save your marriage daily, right from the day you both said 'I DO' in a loving and mutual way.

Note

Note

Note

Note

Note

Note

Note

Note

Note

Note

Note

Note

Printed in Great Britain
by Amazon